Living Beyond
Depression

Living Beyond Depression

by Matilda Nordtvedt

Bethany Fellowship INC.
MINNEAPOLIS, MINNESOTA 55438

Living Beyond Depression

by Matilda Nordtvedt

Library of Congress Catalog Card Number 78-58082

ISBN 0-87123-339-8

DIMENSION BOOKS
Published by Bethany Fellowship, Inc.
6820 Auto Club Road, Minneapolis, Minnesota
55438

Printed in the United States of America

To my 88-year-old mother,
who, in spite of her infirmities,
is usually "on top."

Contents

Introduction

A young man sulks in his room, staring at the walls. Even though he earned a college degree, he cannot function enough to use it.

A middle-aged woman puts on a jolly front when she is with her friends but sobs into her pillow when alone.

A young divorced mother no longer finds meaning for her existence and takes a lethal dose of sleeping pills.

An adolescent boy cannot face his alienation and shoots himself.

These examples are representative of people suffering from depression. There are thousands more.

I understand, because I was one of them. For years I lived part time in the tunnel of depression. Nine years ago I became a permanent resident there. For six long months I stared at the walls, cried into my pillow, found life meaningless, wished to die.

How did I get into such a sorry state? I'm not sure, but I have some ideas.

I also know it's possible to get on top and stay there. I'm just a beginner in this life of victory, but I'd like to share with you in the following chapters what the Holy Spirit has been teaching me. It's exciting, but better yet, it works!

Chapter 1

In and Out of the Tunnel

"O my God, my soul is cast down within me"
(Ps. 42:6).

As I look back toward that dark tunnel, I realize that part of my reason for dwelling there was my lack of self-acceptance. Because I had a low opinion of myself, I assumed others would have a low opinion of me, too. I was the typical overachiever, thinking I had to prove my worth by trying to excel in everything.

As a missionary in Japan, this meant studying the language so diligently that I found myself sleeping in a forest of Japanese words when I went to bed at night. Besides the incessant language study, I tried to assist my husband with his work by helping with the women's group and Sunday school. At the same time I was attempting to be an adequate mother to our three small sons while living in a tiny, inconvenient three-room apartment where we had little privacy from our landlord's family.

After a few years of this I couldn't cope with it all anymore. The doctor said I had "nervous exhaustion" and sent me away for a six-month rest. The rest and tranquilizers brought a measure of relief, but I had lost my zest for living. The years that followed, several more as a missionary and later as a pastor's wife, found me functioning like a teeter-totter—up one day, down the next. Although I seemed normal enough to my friends, I knew and my husband knew that I was tense and nervous much of the time. Often I was depressed. Always I pushed myself too hard and too far, not realizing why I did this.

We had been in our new pastorate in Grand Forks, North Dakota, only a few months when I began to experience "nervous exhaustion" again. Tranquilizers didn't seem to help. Finally the doctor put me in the psychiatric ward of our local hospital. I was there about four weeks, receiving shock treatments, drug therapy and counseling.

When I was released, even though I was labeled "cured," I was severely depressed and still on a heavy dosage of tranquilizers. My husband, at the doctor's suggestion, took me on a trip to Washington and California to visit our families, but I enjoyed very little of it. We came back to Grand Forks and I tried to find fulfillment in my family, my homemaking, the church. But it all seemed meaningless. I was unable to enjoy anything.

I knew that Jesus was my Savior and that I was a child of God, but nothing else made sense. My husband spent hours counseling and comforting me; my sons were considerate; still I was unreasonably depressed, hating to get up in the morning, dragging through a monotonous day, looking forward to evening when I could go to bed and forget my agony in drug-induced oblivion. I found the news on television frightening, the suffering in the world heartbreaking. Life was a hopeless, senseless riddle.

This passionless existence went on for about six months. *Then one evening I made the discovery that changed my life.* I was home alone lying on the davenport reading Hannah Whitall Smith's book, *The Christian's Secret of a Happy Life.* The chapter title, "Is God in Everything?" caught my attention. Mrs. Smith's first sentence is this: "One of the greatest obstacles to an unwavering experience in the interior life is the difficulty of seeing God in everything."[1] She goes on to say that even evils originated against us by Satan cannot reach us without God's knowledge and permission, and by the time they reach us, they become His will for us. Even the sins of others "work together for good to them that love God." Mrs. Smith maintains that seeing God in everything is the only clue to a completely restful life.

That night as I lay on the davenport reading, this truth permeated the darkness of my tunnel. Hope stirred within me. I began to discern meaning in my existence. God showed me that if He is indeed in everything that comes to me, I should give thanks for it all, the hard things as well as the happy ones.

Self-pity had been my constant companion for six months and a regular visitor most of my life before that. How could I keep hobnobbing with her now that God had showed me this wonderful truth of His constant love and care for me? Should I not part company with self-pity and her cohorts—unbelief, pessimism, grumbling and fear? Should I not rather entertain gratitude, faith, hope and optimism?

It should not have been a difficult decision to make, but it was. I had received a morbid kind of satisfaction from my old friends. Was I willing to give up that perverted security? I couldn't knowingly choose to keep them and "see God in everything" at the same time.

Thank God, He gave me grace to turn my back on self-pity and welcome gratitude into my life. My thanksgiving was halting and sporadic at first, but as I continued, it became a way of life for me. God helped me to learn gratefulness to Him not only for obvious blessings of my life but also for what appeared to be the disasters. Could He not also turn the curses into blessings for me as He did with Balaam's curse on Israel? (Neh. 13:2b).

Being thankful for everything also included learning to accept myself as God made me, being grateful even for my limitations. It also meant learning to accept other people the way God made them, in spite of failures and mistakes.

Deliverance from my depression did not happen overnight. At first there was just a glimmer of light in my dark tunnel, but as I obeyed that light (seeing God in everything and thanking Him for everything), I gradually found my way out into the sunshine. Incredible as it may seem, just three weeks after I made this discovery and began praising God, I was out of my tunnel of depression.

I can't thank God enough for His deliverance. Now life makes sense. There's a reason to get up in the morning. I can enjoy simple things again, such as making a meal, taking a walk, visiting with friends, just being alive. These last eight years of freedom have been the happiest of my life.

Of course the devil would like to get me back into that black cave where I am not only miserable but also ineffective as a Christian. Sometimes I listen to him and begin to indulge in self-pity again. Then I remember where that self-pity will lead me—back to that tunnel! I remember that God is in everything that comes to me and that praising Him in every circumstance will bring me the victory. I don't *have* to be depressed anymore. When I begin to thank Him, the devil makes his exit from my thinking.

Sometimes we experience a spiritual victory and great joy in the Lord; we "get on top," psychologically, only to gradually revert to our old ways in the daily routine and pressures of living. The Lord not only intends for us to "get on top," but to stay there, to be consistently victorious.

Chapter 2

Greet the Dawn with Song

"With my song will I praise him" (Ps. 28:7).

During my time of acute depression I greeted each dawn with dread. Worries flooded my mind as soon as I awakened. How could I make it through another weary day? What awful thing might happen to me or to the ones I loved in the unknown day that lay before me? I felt anxious and afraid.

I did not recognize the enemy's voice. I did not realize that I could put him to flight if I greeted the dawn with a song of trust and praise instead of doubt and worry. The psalmist says, "Let us greet the dawn with song" (Ps. 57:8, Living Bible).

After I learned this secret, how different my waking moments became! Before Satan had a chance to plant negative, destructive thoughts in my mind, I began to thank God. The devil can plant his seed of discouragement anywhere except in a thankful heart. As my heart sang a song of praise to Him, doubts and fears crept away to be replaced by faith and joy. I knew it would be a good day no matter what happened.

Throughout the years, men and women of God have put into words and music the songs of the heart. What a blessing these hymns and songs of praise have become. Isaac Watts is called "the father of English hymnody" because he was the first Englishman to introduce hymns of human composure to the church. Many of our best-known hymns are from his pen.

During a crucial battle in the Revolutionary War, a regiment of American soldiers ran out of wadding for their guns. Rev. James Caldwell, an American preacher, rushed into his church, brought out all the hymnbooks and distributed them among the soldiers. Tearing out the pages, the desperate men used them as wadding for their guns while the preacher encouraged them by shouting, "Give 'em Watts, boys! Give 'em Watts!"

Have you tried giving your enemy "Watts" or some other hymn of praise? We may not always sing our song audibly, but if it's there in our hearts, the enemy seeks entrance in vain. Praise routs him every time!

Lettie Cowman, author of *Streams in the Desert* and other helpful devotional books, was almost overwhelmed by exhaustion, sleepless nights and unanswered questions as she cared for her dying husband. She said during these trying days and nights, "The secret of victory is not praying but praising; not asking but thanking." [1]

William Law of the eighteenth century stated, "If anyone would tell you the shortest, surest way to happiness and all perfection, he must tell you to make it a rule to yourself to thank and praise God for everything that happens to you. For it is certain that whatever seeming calamity happens to you, if you thank and praise God for it you will turn it into a blessing."[2]

Laura (not her real name), was suffering from

depression after major surgery. Disturbing thoughts kept her awake at night. The tempter told her she wouldn't be able to go back to sleep, that she would be a wreck the next day and unable to work. She became panicky as she believed she would never get over her nervousness and depression. This only increased her tension and wakefulness. One day a friend gave her a book about praising God for everything. As she began to praise God even during wakeful hours, her emotional state improved. She began to sleep better. After several months of thanksgiving she realized she had conquered her fears and doubts. "It really works to give thanks," she says. "I know, because I tried it."

But how can I praise God when I feel so down in the dumps? We do it in the same way we do anything else that needs to be done: by willing to do so. How many of us feel like going to work on Monday mornings? But we go. How often do we feel like doing the dishes or mowing the lawn? But we do these chores. Often after we begin a task that we had no desire to do, we find ourselves actually enjoying it.

It is the same way with thanksgiving and praise. No, we don't feel like giving thanks when the day is gloomy or when we are confronted with a frustration. But the Bible doesn't say we must *feel* thankful. God says through the inspired writer, "Give thanks." As we obey this command and start to thank God for whatever we are facing, we will find ourselves actually "feeling" thankful as well.

Last fall when I found out that my husband had to undergo open heart surgery, of course I was shocked and deeply concerned. But the words that kept coming to me were: "In everything give thanks." Sometimes it was hard to maintain a thankful attitude. In her book, *Come Away My Beloved*, Frances J. Roberts states that God is saying this to us: "Praise Me. This I ask of thee in times when it seemeth indescribably difficult to do so. I ask it of thee in love that is stern at this point because I know unequivocally that it is your only hope for survival." [3]

I realized this truth during the dark hours before and after my husband's surgery. I have realized it many times since. My only hope for survival in a chaotic, muddled, suffering world is to praise God.

Giving thanks, if persisted in, always results in joy and victory as well as blessing to others. James and Maureen Sundby of Pipestone, North Dakota, experienced this reality. They had planned on a bumper crop in the summer of 1975. To insure good yields they had invested in certified seed for the first time and more fertilizer than usual. That spring heavy rains caused the rivers of North Dakota to overflow their banks. The Sundby's crop was completely obliterated by the flood that resulted. Their large investment of time and money came to nothing!

Fortunately James and Maureen were not only Christians but *praising* Christians. After the initial shock they began to praise God in their loss. A relative visiting them from California was amazed at their attitude. How could they take their calamity so calmly and even joyfully? After she returned to her home she wrote them a letter. "When I saw how you could praise God even when you were flooded out, I knew you had something real. Now I have accepted Christ, too."

Their attitude of praise convinced her of the reality of their Savior.

A friend of mine, Leona Troftgruben, who is a missionary nurse in Cameroun, Africa, felt overwhelmed with work and responsibility. She and a co-worker were manning a dispensary in a remote part of Cameroun. Together with a few African helpers they gave medical aid as well as the gospel message to a great many suffering people. When a meningitis epidemic struck, the girls were swamped with extra work and multiplied problems. To make matters worse, a famine in the north brought a large number of refugees to their area, many of them needing medical help.

Just when Leona felt she couldn't stand the strain of it another day, the mail brought her a book on praising the Lord in every circumstance of life. As Leona began to praise God, her attitude changed. Joy and faith replaced grumbling and self-pity. Her fellow workers noticed her cheerfulness and were encouraged. The patients saw the missionary in a new light as she now joyfully served them. They wondered about her God who gave such strength and joy.

Recently she wrote of new frustrations: dissatisfied national workers, isolation from other missionaries for several months at a time because of flooding during the rainy season, crowds coming for medical aid. But she also wrote about a bird that had been pecking at her window for six days in a row. In it she saw a parable. Did she foolishly peck at the hard windows in her life? She said in conclusion: "I am learning to sing rather than peck at my frustrations." In her prayer notes was this request: "Pray that I will sing as I work and teach."

Yes, singing is the answer. Greet the dawn with a song of praise and keep praising all day long!

A missionary from China told about a Chinese farmer who had been soundly converted. He was so happy in his new faith he kept saying, "Praise the Lord!" all day long. This irritated his unbelieving son. One day he hid his father's Bible, replacing it with a geography book. When the farmer came in from his day's work, he sat down to read his Bible. The Bible was not there, so he opened the geography book instead. Then the son heard his father shout, "Praise the Lord!"

Astonished the son asked, "What do you find to praise the Lord for in my geography book?"

"It says here," answered the father, "that the sea is five miles deep in some places, and the Bible says God has cast my sins into the depths of the sea. My sins are gone forever! Praise the Lord!"

Can we find something to praise God for in a geography book, in a difficult circumstance, frustration, disappointment, tragedy? We can do this only if we really believe what He says, that all things work together for the Christian's good.

The psalmist said, "Let my mouth be filled with thy praise and with thy honour all the day" (Ps. 71:8). "O that men would praise the Lord for his goodness, and for his wonderful works to the children of men!" (Ps. 107:15).

Praising God is the way to stay on top.

Chapter 3

Can't Be Improved Upon

"As for God, his way is perfect . . ." (Ps. 18:30).

I awoke that Wednesday morning with a sense of expectancy. Just one more day and my husband would have his heart surgery. After ten days of anticipating it, what a relief it would be to have it done!

In my devotions that morning, God gave me Psalm 18:30, "As for God, his way is perfect." I meditated on those words. Perfect! That means it couldn't be improved upon.

With the verse ringing in my mind I drove to the hospital to be with my husband this last day before surgery. When I entered his room he said, "Guess what! The doctor says I've got shingles."

I had heard of people having shingles (medically known as herpes zoster). It was a virus disease with eruption of small blisters on the skin along the course of a nerve. Yes, Tom had been complaining about a cluster of blisters on his back, and now they had spread around to one side of his chest. It was irritating and painful. He had already completely lost his appetite after being hospitalized for ten days. And now this? How would it affect his coming surgery?

I began to feel distressed. What would this

mean? Several hours later we found out what it would mean—a delay of at least five days, maybe more, before surgery could be performed.

I found myself asking, "Why, Lord? Why another nerve-racking delay, added discomfort, extra expense, further strain in every way by this complication that You could so easily have prevented?"

His answer came gently but clearly: "As for God, his way is perfect."

My husband had shared this verse and other similar ones with his parishioners many times when they were bewildered about what was happening to them. Now it was his turn and mine to take God at His word.

During the next five days before surgery I was often tempted to complain, yes, even despair, but the words, "As for God, his way is perfect," always brought me back to trust and rest. They helped me to stop questioning. Peace came as I accepted God's will for us. I felt a little awed as I wondered what beautiful design for us was hidden in this disappointment. I did not understand, but it didn't matter. I was trusting Him whose way is *perfect*.

When I was young I was very concerned about finding God's will for my life. I knew it was the only way to go. The more difficult it was, the better I liked it. Now I am older and more cautious. I tend to think of God's way sometimes as a bit risky. What if it means losing my husband? Getting cancer?

I used to worry about these things until one day these words in Psalm 112:7 spoke to me: "He shall not be afraid of evil tidings: his heart is fixed, trusting in the Lord." Evil tidings? How often I had dreaded them. I had played the "what if" game. "What if this awful thing happens to me?"

Now, however, I thought of His great love for me and remembered that He had promised to make everything work together for my good. He was planning for us good things, not bad. I could stop playing the "what if" game, stop dreading the future. Like the psalmist I could say, "O God, my heart is fixed; I will sing and give praise" (Ps. 108:1).

Sometimes we think of God's will only in relation to momentous decisions, such as choosing our vocation, finding a life partner, moving to a new location. We forget that God wants to show us His will in the secondary issues of our lives as well. Life is made up of trifles, including some frustrations, disappointments, irritations. Can we accept these as part of His good, acceptable and perfect will, too? Can we say as Jesus did, "I delight to do thy will, O my God" even when His will is contrary to ours? Can we see that His will is perfect because it is designed to accomplish His purposes in us and through us, and His purposes are always for our best?

Paul says, "In everything give thanks; for this is the will of God in Christ Jesus concerning you" (1 Thess. 5:18). He wants me to thank Him for everything because everything that comes into my life has either been planned or permitted by Him. It is His will and for my good.

Can we say to our Heavenly Father as Jesus did, "Not my will, but thine be done"? Perfection needs no alterations or additions, and His will is perfect.

Sometimes when I awake in the morning and begin to praise God, I am almost overwhelmed with gratitude for His wonderful salvation. I have been forgiven, made His child, and have eternal glory awaiting me. The other morning I began to think of the almost equally great privilege of having the Lord of the universe directing my life, He who knows the end from the beginning. He is ordering my circumstances, the small as well as the great, with a wonderful purpose in mind. And to think that sometimes I rebel and don't let Him have His way!

Thank You, Lord, for Your will which is good, acceptable and perfect in the past, present and future. Accepting it and thanking You for it, even though it may be contrary to mine, I can be victorious.

Chapter 4

The "If Only" Game

"Forgetting those things which are behind" (Phil. 3:13).

While some people play the "what if" game, others concentrate on the "if only" game. The players of the "what if" game constantly fear the future and the terrible things that could happen to them. Consequently worry and dread paralyze them. On the other hand, the players of the "if only" game think constantly of the past. "If only I hadn't done thus and so." "If only I had attained such and such a goal." "If only my loved one were still with me." Longings and regrets incapacitate them.

The "if only-ers" are as full of unbelief as the "what if-ers." The Israelites in the wilderness are a good example. When they didn't have water, they began to play the "if only" game. "Would God that we had died when our brethren died before the Lord!" (Num. 20:3). "If only we had never left Egypt and come to this evil place!" they were murmuring.

Jesus said, "No man, having put his hand to the plough, and looking back, is fit for the kingdom of God" (Luke 9:62). He didn't say *turning* back, but *looking* back. Amy Carmichael, in her book, *Thou Givest, They Gather*, says, "If the plougher, even while his feet are still following the plough, looks anywhere but straight forward, his furrow goes crooked."

There is a place in our lives for nostalgia, but nostalgia out of control is debilitating. Longing for what has been weakens us for the present. A mother whose children have grown up and left home may long for the days when her children were about her. "Those were such beautiful times," she says wistfully. She forgets the piles of diapers, the sleepless nights, the endless work, remembering only the beautiful moments of cuddling her little ones or showing them off to friends.

Solomon said, "Say not thou, What is the cause that the former days were better than these? For thou dost not inquire wisely concerning this" (Ecc. 7:10). Time has a way of erasing unpleasant memories and accentuating good ones. When we long for former days we are not being realistic. We are forgetting the struggles and remembering only the joys. At the same time, we tend to magnify our present struggles and minimize present joys.

Corrie ten Boom in her book, *In My Father's House*, quotes some words of wisdom from her father. When death had taken all the members of their household except him and his two daughters, Mr. ten Boom said, "It's a new life now, Corrie; we must remember the past, but live in anticipation of the future." The three around that oval table at the Beje refused to play the "if only" game. They pressed on to new adventures with God. Soon their house was filled again, this time with missionary children who needed a home while their parents were serving on the mission field. Later when Hitler's forces sought to exterminate the Jews, their house became a refuge for these hunted people. When one chapter in their book of life closed, they joyfully began another.

Not only do longings for what is past weaken us, but so do regrets. Repentance for past sins is essential; regrets are useless. Every person that has ever lived in this world, except Jesus Christ, has failed in some area of his life. For some of us there are many failures. We look back and see how life could have been different if we had been different, if we had followed the Lord and His Word fully.

God knows all about our failures. The psalmist said, "O God, thou knowest my foolishness, and my sins are not hidden from thee" (Ps. 69:5). He also says, "But there is forgiveness with thee" (Ps. 130:4). The Lord promises to blot out our sins, cast them into the depths of the sea.

Let's be done then with regrets, "Forgetting those things which are behind, and reaching forth unto those things which are before" (Phil. 3:13). Let's stop playing the "if only" game. It will only bring us heartache and defeat.

Let's accept what we cannot change, not reluctantly but joyfully. Let's look back only to praise Him for His forgiveness, His faithfulness, His guidance through the years. Let's look forward with trust and confidence, get on top of our "if only's."

Chapter 5

God Did It

"Thou hast caused men to ride over our heads" (Ps. 66:12).

I had been slighted. How could people be so unkind and thoughtless? By now I knew that retreating to the tunnel and commiserating with self-pity was not the way to go. I turned to the Lord and His Word instead. My Bible reading for that day was Psalm 66.

Imagine my surprise when I read the words, "Thou broughtest us into the net; thou laidst affliction upon our loins. Thou hast caused men to ride over our heads; we went through fire and through water" (66:11, 12).

I took a deep breath. "You, Lord?" I asked. "You caused this hurt? How could You?"

Bewildered, I read on: " . . . but thou broughtest us out into a wealthy place." A wealthy place? Enrichment? Through the insults of people?

My mind flew back to the previous morning—before I had been hurt. I had read my Bible and prayed as usual, but I didn't get much out of it. I was too self-satisfied, too absorbed with things of earth. I hadn't had much appetite for the eternal.

But now I fairly gobbled up the verses before me. I set out to memorize the entire psalm. It blessed me over and over again for weeks. A wealthy place? Yes, the Lord had brought me into great spiritual wealth and blessing. How? Through "causing men to ride over my head."

The disciples, bewildered at the turn of events after Jesus' resurrection and missing His constant presence with them, had gone out fishing. But in spite of their best efforts they caught nothing all night long. In the morning they saw a man standing on the shore. He called to them, "Children, have you any food?" They didn't realize the man was Jesus.

Jesus told them that if they cast the nets on the right side of the boat they would find fish. They did, and immediately their net was full to overflowing. Suddenly John realized who was standing on the shore, who had filled their nets. "It is the Lord!" he exclaimed. Simon Peter jumped into the sea to swim to Him.

How often we, like the disciples, recognize the Lord when our nets are full of fish. We see evidence of His love and blessing and say happily, "It is the Lord who has done all this for me." But in times of disappointment and frustration we don't recognize Him. Jesus walks to us on the sea of our trouble and says, "Be of good cheer. It is I; be not afraid" (Mark 6:50). He says, "I am permitting this difficulty, this frustration, this illness, this misunderstanding, this tragedy. It is part of my glorious plan for you. Recognize Me in it. Be of good cheer! Don't be afraid!"

Madame Guyon saw God in all of her trials. A Catholic woman of the seventeenth century who was used of God to awaken decadent France, Madame Guyon was probably the most misunderstood woman in history.

Her father chose for her to marry at the age of fifteen a man twenty-two years her senior. The man's mother, with whom they lived, proved to be an extremely disagreeable and unreasonable woman. Although the husband allegedly loved his beautiful young wife, as time went on he sided more and more with his mother against her. The maid assigned to be her aid added her ill-temper and abuse to the constant scoldings of the mother-in-law and husband. Madame Guyon could do nothing to please any of them.

Yet she did not become resentful or bitter. She realized that these trials were necessary for her spiritual growth. An extremely beautiful girl, she had been admired and desired by many. She recognized the pride of her heart because of her beauty and grieved much over it. Perhaps these humiliations in the house of her husband would help her to die to her proud and haughty nature.

One day when returning from a trip, she learned that during her absence the dreaded disease of smallpox had invaded her home. Her oldest son and youngest daughter were desperately ill. Friends urged her to go to stay with her father so she would not catch the disease which so often in those days proved fatal. She wished to do so but her mother-in-law would not hear of it.

Madame Guyon stayed as her mother-in-law demanded and did indeed come down with smallpox. Her mother-in-law stubbornly refused to send for a doctor until it was almost too late. She was desperately ill for three weeks, but God spared her life. One child died from the disease, but her oldest son recovered.

One day he came in to see his mother. She gasped in dismay when she saw him. His face that

had been so handsome was now disfigured by ugly
pock marks. Looking into a mirror at herself she discovered that the same thing had happened to her. Her
beauty was gone!

Madame Guyon did not become resentful but
accepted this as God's perfect plan for her. She
could have blamed her mother-in-law for exposing
her to the disease, but instead she said: "God
makes use of creatures, and their natural inclina-
tions to accomplish His designs. When I see in the
creatures a conduct which appears unreasonable
and mortifying, I mount higher, and look upon
them as instruments both of the mercy and justice
of God." [1]

After her husband's death, Madame Guyon
was free to engage in religious and charitable activities as much as she pleased. She was severely
criticized for sharing her wealth with charitable
organizations. She was falsely accused of immoral
designs. Her writings, which God used to lead
many into a closer walk with Him, were condemned
by her church. Finally she was imprisoned.

She said when persecuted, "Loving the strokes
which God gives, one cannot hate the hand which
He makes use of to strike with." [2]

In prison she sang praises to God. She said,
"The stones of my prison looked in my eyes like
rubies: I esteemed them more than all the gaudy
brilliancies of a vain world. My heart was full of
that joy which Thou givest to them who love Thee,
in the midst of their greatest crosses." [3] At another
time she stated that her greatest cross would be to
be without a cross.

Madame Guyon died in prison at the age of 70
but her writings remain to bless and inspire those
who will take time to read them. If she had not

recognized God's hand in her trials, if she had not accepted everything as His permissive will, she probably would have broken down years before under the strain of her maltreatment. She would have been a self-pitying neurotic instead of a victorious Christian rising above all the misunderstanding, malignment and persecution hurled at her.

Madame Guyon believed that "God did it." As the psalmist in Psalm 66, she realized that He was the One who had caused men to ride over her head. He was the One that allowed the afflictions to come. And for what purpose? To bring her out into a *wealthy* place, a place of spiritual enrichment and usefulness.

Perhaps you feel that such an attitude is demeaning, equivalent to allowing yourself to become a doormat to be stepped upon. To the contrary, it is an exalted position. When we "get even" with those who offend us, we do just that, lower ourselves to their level of baseness. When we take their insults to us as permitted by God and thank Him for them, we become the master of the situation. The offender actually becomes our servant to help us rise to new heights.

There is much misunderstanding in our world. Many are hurting because of someone's thoughtlessness or even cruelty. Solomon says, "The spirit of a man will sustain his infirmity; but a wounded spirit who can bear?" (Prov. 18:14).

In other words, having a wounded spirit is worse than suffering from a physical malady. We all know people who must endure constant physical suffering but maintain a cheerful, rejoicing spirit. On the other hand, we know people who have nothing wrong with them physically, but they are miserable and make others around them miserable because they are nursing a wounded spirit.

We all get hurt by others. Nearly all of us are sensitive when it comes to slights, being ignored, being criticized. Some people, like Madame Guyon, have to endure *severe* abuse and mistreatment. We can react with resentment and self-pity or we can take it all as permitted by the Lord, forgive and forget.

One dear Christian woman I know who has suffered much, chose the latter. She refuses to even think about the wrongs done to her. She has taken them to the Lord, and forgiven those who wronged her. As a result she is living a happy, victorious, God-glorifying life.

On the other hand, I know a Christian man who suffered an injustice which he refuses to accept as part of God's training for him. He doesn't even see God in it, only the people who have hurt him. What in the beginning was like a small scratch has developed into an ugly wound. A wounded spirit is depriving him of his peace and fellowship with other Christians. It is causing untold damage to those around him as well as to himself.

Dr. S. I. McMillen says in his excellent book, *None of These Diseases,* that ulcerative colitis, toxic goiters, high blood pressure are a few of the scores of diseases caused by bitterness. When we become resentful our pituitary, adrenal, thyroid and other glands give forth certain hormones, which cause diseases in the body.[4] A wounded, unforgiving spirit can result in physical diseases as well as spiritual deterioration.

Lecturer Bill Gothard advises that instead of becoming bitter when wronged, we view the offender as a tool of God. God is using that tool to chip away our rough edges and to make us into something that can reflect His beauty.

Have you been wounded? Don't strike back. Don't mull over it. Take it to the Lord. Recognize that He is in control. He did it, or permitted it, not to hurt you but to teach you some valuable lesson you could not have learned otherwise.

If you have been feeling sorry for yourself and nursing your wound, confess your self-pity to the Lord (it is sin, you know). Forgive from your heart the one who has wounded you. Go a step farther and thank God for the wound and the one who inflicted it. Thank Him, too, for the spiritual wealth you are going to derive from this experience. Thank Him for the new sympathy it has given you for others who are wounded, perhaps by you, and for the opportunity to avail yourself of His grace in forgiving the one who has offended you.

We can overcome our hurts!

Chapter 6

God's Point of View

"For as the heavens are higher than the earth, so are my ways higher than your ways, and my thoughts than your thoughts" (Isa. 55:9).

Rev. and Mrs. Wendell Johnson in Dalton, Minnesota, eagerly anticipated the birth of their fifth child. They already had four fine boys. Wouldn't it be great to get a girl?

The baby was a girl, but a Downs Syndrome (Mongoloid) child. What a crushing blow! What a tragedy! Or, at least so it seemed to us, looking at it from a human point of view. To God it was not a tragedy. It was part of His plan for this family, part of His wonderful purpose. Who knows what great things He will accomplish in this family and in many others through this little handicapped girl?

When Charles Cowman, missionary to Japan, became ill and had to return to the States, his wife, Lettie, was sure that the Lord would heal him and permit him to return to his work on the mission field. But Mr. Cowman's condition only became worse. Day after day he languished and night after night he suffered until at last he died.

After her husband's death Lettie Cowman wrote in her diary, "I must look at the glory side."[1] In other words, she must look at her great sorrow and loss from God's perspective.

Oh, yes, there is a "glory side" to every problem, affliction, perplexity, misunderstanding and loss. It is God's point of view. When we look at things the way He does, our suffering becomes a servant, our trials become treasures, our loss becomes gain, and our pain becomes blessing.

Watchman Nee, Chinese Christian scholar, discovered something disturbing in his ministry. The people to whom he was ministering had become Christians. They had accepted Jesus Christ by faith, received forgiveness of sins and eternal life. When they met together on Sundays they rejoiced in the fact that their guilt was gone and their eternal destiny assured. They also rejoiced in the comfort God gave them during times of trouble and trial. But they seemed to have no desire to go beyond this. Between their religious activities on Sundays their thinking resembled that of their heathen neighbors.

Satan seeks to gain control of the Christian's thoughts. It doesn't bother him too much if the Christian is living a respectable life, going to church and taking part in religious activities as long as he can get him to think like a man of the world, between Sundays.

Elisabeth Elliot in her book, *These Strange Ashes,* states: "We are not by nature inclined to think spiritually. We are ready to assign almost any other explanation to the things that happen to us. There is a certain reticence to infer that our little troubles may actually be the vehicles to bring us to God."[2]

There is only one way to see things from God's perspective and that is to saturate our minds with

38

His Word. His thinking is opposite from man's. Man says, "Assert yourself"; God says, "Humble yourself." Man says, "Demand your rights"; God says, "Go an extra mile." Man says, "Get even with your enemies"; God says, "Love and forgive your enemies." Man says, "Get all you can for yourself"; God says, "Give all you can, even yourself." Man says, "Pity yourself"; God says, "Give thanks for all things."

In God's Word we find God's thoughts, His perspective. We discover His exceeding great and precious promises. We see the "glory side" to our problems.

Job said, "I have esteemed the words of his mouth more than my necessary food" (Job 23:12). That's the way I felt about my Bible during the trying days before, during and after my husband's open heart surgery. God's Word became my meat and drink. Before I went to the hospital every morning I spent time memorizing and meditating on key portions that I knew would sustain me during the day.

Most of the women in the hospital family waiting room, ministering to their ill loved ones, had a good cry once in a while. I'd come upon them in the restroom, and quickly retreat so they could give vent to their emotions in private.

I had my cries, too, when the strain and tension just seemed too much. But invariably my crying spells ended in a time of praise and thanksgiving to God, because He comforted me with His Word that I had stored in my memory.

One day when I was about to indulge in a session of self-pity, God's Word came to my rescue. (I was memorizing Psalm 91 at the time.) "He that dwelleth in the secret place of the most High shall abide under the shadow of the Almighty."

I was comforted as I realized that although I was spending every day at the hospital, I was really "dwelling in the secret place of the most High." Imagine such a dwelling place! I was awed as I realized that in spite of outward distresses my husband and I were "under the shadow of the Almighty." As I pondered the words I felt too privileged to feel sorry for myself any longer. Those words lifted me up and changed my entire outlook for that day. I found myself rejoicing and praising. Yes, I found the "glory side."

I was reminded to be satisfied with my surroundings by the verse in 1 Timothy 6:8, "And having food and raiment, let us be therewith content." I thought of that as I took my place in line at the hospital cafeteria every day. Certainly I would rather be at home cooking my own food, but this was God's provision for now, and He wanted me to be content with it.

"All the paths of the Lord are mercy and truth unto such as keep his covenant and his testimonies" from Psalm 25 encouraged me to rejoice in His ways even though they were different from my choosing.

Shortly before my husband was hospitalized I dented a woman's station wagon while backing out of a parking place at the supermarket. A few months before this I had hit a car while pulling out of a parallel parking place in a hurry. These incidents made me extremely nervous about driving, especially at night. I was almost ready to give it up altogether.

While in Fargo, however, I had no choice but to drive to and from the place where I stayed. I quaked at the thought of driving in a strange city, especially at night. What a desolate feeling engulfed me each evening as I left my husband's bedside and walked out to the car. How I prayed as I guided the car out of the crowded parking lot and started down the unfamiliar streets. I breathed a sigh of relief when I reached my destination, but there was still the parking problem. Remembering the dents, I cautiously started backing into what seemed like an impossibly small space, praying fervently all the while. The verse that came to mind and gave me courage was: "He shall give his angels charge over thee, to keep thee in all thy ways . . . lest at any time thou *dent the car behind thee* [my paraphrase]" (Ps. 91:11, 12). I couldn't see the angel sitting on the front fender and the one on the back one, but from God's Word I knew they were there.

I can say with the psalmist, "Unless thy law had been my delights, I should then have perished in mine affliction" (Ps. 119:92). At least I would have been terribly frustrated!

I was challenged to memorize Scripture by reading *In the Presence of Mine Enemies* by Howard Rutledge.[3] Shot down over North Viet Nam, Captain Rutledge was taken prisoner by the Viet Cong. For six long years he suffered in a Communist prison camp, much of that time in solitary confinement. The most important thing in Captain Rutledge's life during those long, agonizing days and nights in prison was God and His Word. His greatest delight was to reconstruct in his mind verses of Scripture and hymns he had learned in Sunday school as a boy. The other American prisoners were just as eager for God's Word as Rutledge was. The biggest highlight of a day was when someone recalled a verse from

Scripture or the line of a hymn and shared it with the others by means of a code tapped on the cell wall with a tin cup. When solitary confinement became unbearable, Captain Rutledge would pace back and forth in his small cell repeating God's Word and softly singing hymns. By this means he retained his sanity and was able to withstand the brainwashing of the enemy.

The Psalmist said he rejoiced in the Word of God as much as in all riches (Ps. 119:14). He claimed it was better to him than thousands of gold and silver (Ps. 119:72). God's Word had done so much for him—that's why he made such extravagant statements about it. He elaborates in Psalm 119. God's Word cleansed him, kept him from sin, counseled him, gave him liberty, gave him hope, gave him comfort, gave him life, gave him delight, gave him strength, gave him a song, gave him wisdom, gave him more understanding than his teachers, gave him great peace that nothing could disturb; it was his light and the rejoicing of his heart.

David cried out, "Oh, how love I thy law! It is my meditation all the day!" (Ps. 119:97).

Cleansing, victory over sin, counsel, liberty, hope, comfort, strength, wisdom, understanding, a song, joy, light and peace are all waiting for the believer in the Word of God.

Years ago in Europe it was against the law to own and read the Bible. Believers buried their Bibles in the earth, taking them out in the middle of the night to read secretly by candlelight.

Today in some Communist countries Bibles are so scarce portions are copied by hand to be distributed among the Christians. Even pastors of some underground churches in Russia do not own a complete copy of God's Word.

Amos prophesied, "Behold, the days come, saith the Lord God, that I will send a famine in the land, not a famine of bread, not a thirst for water, but of hearing the words of the Lord: and they shall wander from sea to sea, and from the north even to the east, they shall run to and fro to seek the word of the Lord, and shall not find it" (Amos 8:11, 12).

If we hide scripture in our hearts, we won't need to fear the coming famine of the Word of God. We won't be desolate even if our Bibles are taken from us. We may not always be privileged to have a Bible in our hands, but we can have it in our hearts.

Memorizing God's Word has become such a help to me. It's right there when I need it, ready for the Holy Spirit to use to rebuke, instruct, encourage, strengthen or comfort. It's the best way I know to see things from God's point of view, the "glory side," to *stay on top*.

Chapter 7

Take Off Your Dark Glasses

"For he endured, as seeing him who is invisible"
(Heb. 11:27).

When I put on my dark glasses, everything becomes a different color. Sometimes I forget I have them on. I get used to seeing everything looking darker than it actually is. Often my spiritual outlook is clouded by the dark glasses of unbelief.

The writer of Hebrews says, "Take heed, brethren, lest there be in any of you an evil heart of unbelief, in departing from the living God" (Heb. 3:12).

Unbelief begins when we substitute our natural reasoning for God's Word. God promises to make all things work together for our good. He commands us to thank Him in *everything*. Instead, we often put on the dark glasses of doubt, then wonder why everything looks so dark.

Not only do these glasses make everything look dark, they actually distort our view. Can you imagine anyone calling Egypt, the place of slavery, a "land that floweth with milk and honey"? That was God's description of the Promised Land, not Egypt. Dathan and Abiram, with distorted vision, said to Moses, "Is it a small thing that thou hast brought us up out of a land that floweth with milk and honey, to kill us in the wilderness . . . ?" (Num. 16:13).

How could Dathan and Abiram be so blind? Had they so quickly forgotten the hard bondage under which they were made to serve in Egypt? Had they so quickly forgotten the marvelous Red Sea deliverance and the other miracles God had performed for them? How could they call cruel bondage "milk and honey"?

What clouded the vision of these men and made them believe a lie? Unbelief. They didn't trust God's love and wisdom in His dealings with them. They refused to be content in their circumstances, to thank God for what He had done for them and what He was going to do. They thought they were criticizing Moses and Aaron, but they were really criticizing God. They were really saying, "Lord, why did You give us these leaders? Why did You put me in these circumstances?"

God's judgment against these three men and those they had influenced, shows us what He thinks of our dissatisfaction with what He has planned for us. He caused the earth to open up and swallow them!

The remaining Israelites should have gotten the message—should have understood the gravity of complaining against God and His servants, but they didn't. The next day they gathered together in rebellion against Moses and Aaron and murmured saying, "Ye have killed the people of the Lord" (Num. 16:41). Again, unbelief had darkened their minds. Instead of seeing their own sin, they blamed Moses and Aaron. The dark glasses of unbelief usually work that way. Instead of searching our own hearts, we blame others for our predicaments. Instead of realizing that our circumstances and our associates are part of God's plan for us, we grumble and complain.

We think of complaining as a negligible sin or perhaps no sin at all. Yet when the Israelites murmured against Moses because of the wilderness diet and other hardships, it displeased the Lord (Numbers 11). He *heard* the murmurings. They were directed to Moses and Aaron but were actually against God (Exodus 16). God called their complaints "despising the Lord" (Num. 11:20).

How can my complaining be "despising the Lord"? It is actually saying to Him, "You're mistreating me. You don't know what's best for me. You don't love me." Or worse still it is saying, "God doesn't have anything to do with my circumstances. He's not in control."

Our farmer friend (I'll call him Hank) was worried. Weather conditions had caused his potatoes to turn out sub-standard. They wouldn't bring the income that he had anticipated. Maybe they wouldn't even bring enough cash to pay for the seed. What about his bills, the living expenses for him and his family?

Thinking these gloomy thoughts he began to haul his potatoes to the warehouse. He felt ready to explode with agitation and anger. Even the traffic lights seemed to work against him. Suddenly, as he waited for a light to turn green, a verse of scripture flashed into his mind: ". . . Whatsoever things are true, whatsoever things are honest, whatsoever things are just, whatsoever things are pure, whatsoever things are lovely, whatsoever things are of good report; if there be any virtue, and if there be any praise, think on these things" (Phil. 4:8).

The Holy Spirit convicted Hank of his

pessimistic, gloomy, dark thoughts. Hank began to deliberately concentrate on good things as the verse directed. In other words, he took off his dark glasses. Gratitude replaced his anger as he thought of God's goodness and blessings. He turned his situation over to God and relaxed. Later he found out that his potatoes weren't as poor as he had imagined and although they brought less than he had hoped, he realized a profit sufficient to take care of his needs. Most important of all, he learned to trust instead of doubt.

Reading Luke 12, about God's care for the sparrows and the lilies and His much greater concern for us, will help us to take off those dark glasses of unbelief. We who know the Lord have the greatest power of the universe on our side. "And if God be for us, who can be against us?" (Rom. 8:32). We could add, "*What* can be against us?"

It's looking brighter already, isn't it!

Chapter 8

Thought Control

"Bringing into captivity every thought to the obedience of Christ" (2 Cor. 10:5).

A few years ago Associated Press Staff writer, John Barbour, discussed in a series of articles the subject of mind control. He told of a highly disturbed man being able to control his feelings by pushing the button on a little black box fastened around his waist which sent an electrical current to his brain. Immediately dark, angry feelings were replaced by pleasant ones. Much research has been done on controlling the emotions and mental processes of mentally disturbed people with electrical currents. The danger of the misuse of these discoveries, however, outweighs the good they could do.

Drugs are also being used as mood changers. Once when I was feeling overly tired, a doctor gave me some pills that gave me great bursts of energy. I cleaned our entire basement with great enthusiasm, a chore I usually disliked doing, and, when I had finished, I didn't even feel tired. I felt as jolly as Santa Claus, joking and laughing all day. My children thought they had a new mother. One day of that artificial happiness was enough for me. Suspicious of anything in a bottle that could change me so drastically, I flushed the rest of the pills down the toilet.

I have discovered a way to change my mood, however, quite apart from electrodes and anti-depressant pills. I have discovered that I can control the *thoughts* that control my moods.

In March of 1974 Mrs. Eunice Kronholm, a banker's wife from St. Paul, Minnesota, was kidnapped and held for ransom. The kidnapped woman, a Christian, realized during her ordeal the importance of controlling her thoughts.

What would you think about if you were blindfolded for four days, guarded by nervous, desperate criminals? What thoughts would go through your mind as you jolted about for eight hours in the trunk of a car, not knowing where you were being taken?

Mrs. Kronholm could have panicked, but she didn't because she kept her thoughts, not on her desperate situation, but on God. As a teacher of psychology, she had often told her nurses that they could control their thoughts. Now she had a chance to prove it.

Have you ever been in an intolerable situation, about to go to pieces and said to yourself, "This isn't as bad as I *think* it is; my negative thoughts are making it far worse than it is"?

I've never been kidnapped or been kept captive in the trunk of a car. In less dramatic situations, however, I have experienced the power of thoughts. The other day I felt ready to explode. I knew that the only way I could be relieved of my agitation was to "blow my top" at the person involved. At the same time I knew that wasn't God's way and would only lead to more strife and hard feelings. Finally, reluctantly at first, I committed

49

the matter to the Lord. I decided to let Him take care of it instead of trying to solve it in a carnal way.

I was amazed at the change that took place in me when I surrendered my thinking to Him and let Him take control. My agitation vanished. The grievance suddenly seemed quite small and insignificant. As I watched Him work it out so beautifully I thanked Him over and over again for reminding me to let Him control my thinking and my subsequent actions.

It boils down to this: I am what I think; I do what I think. My thoughts are powerful for either good or bad. I have a choice: to let my thinking be controlled by my old sinful nature or to let the Holy Spirit control it. Paul speaks of "bringing into captivity every thought to the obedience of Christ" (2 Cor. 10:5). This is not automatic. We must *will* to be controlled. We must *yield* ourselves to His control.

We can think negative, destructive thoughts or we can think positive, uplifting ones. We can think thoughts of self-pity or thoughts of thankfulness. We can think hopeless thoughts or let the "God of hope fill [us] with all joy and peace in believing" (Rom. 15:13).

How we think makes all the difference in whether we're down or whether we're on top.

Chapter 9

Questions, Questions

"Blessed is he whosoever shall not be offended in me" (Luke 7:23).

Some things in life are impossible to understand. Elisabeth Elliot, young missionary to Ecuador, tells in her book, *These Strange Ashes*, about some of her perplexities. Her first assignment when she arrived on the mission field was to reduce the language of the Colorado Indians to writing so they could eventually have God's Word in their own tongue.

Many things went wrong. Besides the difficulties of jungle living, Elisabeth and her co-workers experienced one crushing disappointment after another. Maruja, a member of one of the most resistant families in the area, died in childbirth, in spite of the best efforts and prayers of the young missionaries. It was like losing the key that could have opened up an entire tribe to the Gospel.

The second great tragedy was the murder of Elisabeth's language informant, the only one in the area who knew both the Colorado and Spanish languages, the only one who could help her in reducing the language to writing, he who had been God's answer to her prayers.

The third tragedy struck after Elisabeth had completed the phonetic and phonemic alphabet of the Colorado language. Her months of painstaking work had resulted in a language file which would enable fellow missionaries to carry on the translation while Elisabeth went to a new place of service prior to her marriage to Jim Elliot.

Imagine her consternation when she learned some months later that the language materials, stored in a suitcase, had been stolen! Nine months of hard work come to nothing! Or so it seemed. Why? Why? Why?

Amy Carmichael tells about an Indian girl in her book, *Mimosa*. Mimosa knew very little about the true God except that He loved her and in every least thing would wonderfully lead her. With unwavering faith in these two glorious facts she triumphed over every obstacle that came to her.

When Mimosa's precious second son died, her neighbors accused her of causing his death by forsaking the gods of India. Mimosa's faith did not flinch. She said to her God, "I am not offended with You."

The next calamity that struck was the death of the family bull, and that just when they were beginning to prosper. At first Mimosa was perplexed, but not for long. If the bull had lived and they had continued to prosper, perhaps she would have forgotten God and the things that mattered most. Why should she lament? Was not God in every least thing wonderfully leading her? She would not be offended with Him.

Miss Hosogawa of Northern Japan eagerly looked forward to beginning a Christian witness in the city of Morioka. Just out of Bible school and full of vision, she went to the city far from her own home to prepare the way for a missionary couple who would follow in a few months.

The young Japanese Christian met disappointment and frustration almost immediately. She became seriously ill with pneumonia and had to be hospitalized. Imagine her desolate feeling, alone in a strange city, far from home, failing in the work she had been sent to accomplish. Bewildered, she asked, "Why, God? I came here to work for You. Why did You permit this illness, this hospitalization?"

As Miss Hosogawa searched her Bible for the answer to her question she came upon Romans 8:28 which states that "all things work together for good to them that love God." But how could this illness which was preventing her from her work for the Lord be good?

The head nurse saw Miss Hosogawa reading her Bible and asked her to speak to a patient who had tried to commit suicide. The young Christian began to see a plan in the puzzle as she gave God's Word to this troubled woman.

Word got around that Miss Hosogawa was a Christian. One of the doctors came to talk to her. "I, too, am a Christian," he said. "My wife and I spent many years in Taiwan and have just recently moved to Morioka. We would like to become involved in Christian work."

Miss Hosogawa was overjoyed. Here was the help they needed to start their church. Dr. and Mrs. Sasaki were the answer to her prayers. They had been brought together through her pneumonia which she had considered a disaster, but was actually part of a beautiful plan.

How wise God is! But how often we forget. Sometimes, like Hosogawa, we can see God working out His plan through our difficulties and disappointments. Sometimes, however, the good that God has promised to work out through "all things" is not obvious to us. Like Elisabeth Elliot we are perplexed, bewildered by the unexplainable.

Paul said, "How unsearchable are his judgments, and his ways past finding out!" Or, as the Living Bible puts it, "How impossible it is for us to understand his decisions and his methods!" (Rom. 11:33). The psalmist said, "Your decisions are as full of wisdom as the oceans are with water" (Ps. 36:6, Living Bible).

In the movie, "The Hiding Place," the suffering women of the Ravensbruck Concentration Camp asked questions of Betsie and Corrie, who, in spite of everything, maintained their faith in God. If God was a God of love, why did He allow such suffering? If He had power, why didn't He do something to allay their misery? Sometimes Betsie and Corrie didn't know the answers, but through it all they believed in the love and wisdom of their God. They were not offended in Him.

Flannery O'Conner, famous novelist, said, "One of the tendencies of our age is to use suffering of children to discredit the goodness of God, and once you have discredited His goodness, you are done with Him." [1] When we insist upon asking, "Why?" about suffering, we are discrediting God's goodness. We are thinking like unbelievers.

Elisabeth Elliot said, "Faith's most severe tests come not when we see nothing, but when we see a stunning array of evidence that seems to prove our faith vain. . . . It was a long time before I came to the realization that it is in our acceptance of what is given that God gives Himself." [2]

When we read of the heroes of faith in Hebrews 11 we see that God miraculously delivered some of them: from the sword, from lions, from fire, from violence. Yet in the midst of this recital of miraculous deliverances we also read: "But others were tortured . . . had trial of cruel mockings and scourgings, yea, moreover of bonds and imprisonment. They were stoned, they were sawn asunder, were tested, were slain with the sword . . . of whom the world was not worthy" (Heb. 11:35-38). Why were some delivered and others not? Only heaven will reveal the answer to these perplexities.

Shadrach, Meshach and Abednego had the right attitude when they faced death in the fiery furnace. They said to King Nebuchadnezzar, " . . . Our God, whom we serve, is able to deliver us from the burning fiery furnace, and he will deliver us out of thine hand, O king. *But if not*, be it known unto thee, O king, that we will not serve thy gods, nor worship the golden image which thou hast set up" (Dan. 3:17, 18).

But if not! How I love those three little words. They mean that I will not be offended no matter what God lets happen to me. It means I will trust God's wisdom even when I cannot understand. I will accept instead of question.

So often we question God's dealings with us. "Why did my husband lose his job? Why is my child handicapped? Why did we get involved in a terrible car accident? Why did my loved one die?"

We also question God about small matters. "Why did You let company come today when I was in the middle of waxing my floor? Why did the washing machine break today of all days? Why can't I get the car started? Why doesn't the baby go to sleep so I can get my work done? Why is my boss so unreasonable today? Why must I suffer wakeful hours at night?"

I found myself questioning God during the weeks at home following my husband's heart surgery. The doctor told him that in six to eight weeks he could be back at work again. Soon he would feel better than he had for years. But it didn't work out that way. We were glad to be home after four weeks in the hospital, but we missed the reassurance of the nurses and doctors. My husband had pains in his chest that he could not understand. He didn't gain his strength as quickly as he had hoped. Visitation and counseling made him exhausted and at the same time too agitated to sleep. Many nights were long—scary, as we asked questions. "Why doesn't he get better? Is there something else wrong?" After he had been taking long walks outside for several weeks, the doctor restricted him to the house and complete rest again. We were confused, bewildered. I began to get pains in my chest from tension. We found ourselves questioning, "Why, Lord?"

God asks us questions, too. Jesus said to His disciples, "O ye of little faith, why reason ye among yourselves?" (Matt. 16:8). He said to His disciples during the storm, "Why are ye fearful, O ye of little faith?" (Matt. 8:26). He said to Peter when he began to sink after walking on the water, "Why didst thou doubt?" (Matt. 14:31). He said when the disciples awakened Him during the storm on the lake, "Where is your faith?" (Luke 8:25). He asks us, "Why are ye anxious?" (Matt. 6:28).

When Watchman Nee was leaving England after being invited to speak there, he said, "You people have wonderful light, but oh so little faith." [3] Could he have said the same about us American Christians?

When Charles Spurgeon was visiting a farmer friend one day he noticed the words "God is Love" written underneath the weathervane.

"Does that mean that God's love is as changeable as the wind?" someone asked.

"No," answered the farmer, "it means that God is love no matter how the wind blows."

Lord, forgive me for always asking, "Why?" Help me to believe You, to trust even when I do not understand. Instead of questioning You, help me to *praise* You, knowing that what You are permitting in my life and doing for me is for my highest good, knowing that in every least thing you are wonderfully leading me. Lord, I will not be offended in You.

Chapter 10

No Biggee

"There is really only one thing worth being concerned about" (Luke 10:42, Living Bible).

When our youngest son worked at a local drive-in restaurant during his high school days, he came home with the expression learned from his boss, "No biggee." When I asked him what it meant, Mark shrugged. "No sweat—no big deal."

Sometimes when I get all tensed up over a situation I think of those words, "No biggee." Is what I am upset about big enough to merit my getting upset? This year's Christmas letters is an example. I was so frustrated, wondering how I could possible get them all out on time. My husband assured me that I didn't even have to send Christmas letters, much less get all shook up about them.

I asked myself the question, "What would happen if I didn't get the letters out on time or even not at all? Would I be shot at dawn? Would my husband stop loving me? Would I lose my place in God's eternal kingdom?" The answer was "no" three times. As soon as I realized that it was really "no biggee," I was able to relax about it. I got them all out in record time without nervous prostration!

Last summer my newly converted sister-in-law taught me a valuable lesson. Very early in her Christian life she had learned to "fret not." Every time an irritation came up she would say cheerfully, "Remember, fret not!"

But it's easy for me to fret—not so much over the large crises of life but at the small, aggravating frustrations.

The plums I canned from the tree in our backyard, using expensive sugar, scarce lids and precious time turned out sour! My disposition was about to turn sour, too. Then I remembered: "Fret not! No biggee!" I was amazed to find that the sour plums didn't have to destroy my peace and rob me of my tranquillity.

I thought about my position as a Christian, my riches and inheritance in Christ, my eternal destiny. What difference, really, did a few jars of sour plums make? Why should I get flustered and make myself and others miserable? It was "no biggee."

Often I have to tell myself this in my relationships with my family and friends. Maybe one of them is short with me. I feel hurt, slighted. I should stop and tell myself right away, "It's no biggee. He's probably tired, preoccupied with problems, having a struggle over something." How easy it is instead to make an oversight into a huge misunderstanding. Invariably if I do, I ask myself afterwards with much regret, "Why was I so stupid? Why did I make a 'biggee' out of something so trivial and insignificant?"

A district attorney stated that fully half of the cases in criminal courts originate in little things. Domestic wrangling, an insulting remark, a disparaging word, a rude action—these are the things that often lead to assault and murder. It is these little blows to our self-esteem which we magnify out of proportions that cause so much heartache in the world.

Trivialities are at the bottom of most marital problems, too. We take a hasty word, a cross look, a brief gruffness as a personal affront when often it is not meant that way. As we dwell on our little hurts they grow big like a snowball rolled over and over in the snow.

One night I fussed and stewed because we were unavoidably delayed for a dinner engagement. I fretted the whole ten miles and fifteen minutes it took us to get there. To my relief our hostess was not a bit disturbed. "It's good you were late," she said when we apologized, "because I'm behind schedule today and dinner isn't ready." And I had worked myself up into such a dither over it!

Britisher R.V.C. Bodley in his book, *In Search of Serenity*, tells of leaving his diplomatic post to spend seven years in the Sahara living with the Arabs. One of the main things he learned from the Arabs was the futility of fussing about something over which you have no control. When things went wrong these men of the desert never became nervous, anxious or excited. They merely shrugged and said, "In sha Allah"—"if God so wills." [1]

Martha of the Bible was a fusser. Efficient, ambitious people often are. Here she was bustling around to prepare a perfect meal for Jesus while her sister Mary sat and listened to the Master.

(I know the feeling. Everything needs to be done at once and you have only two hands. How can you mash the potatoes, cut the meat, make the gravy, and put the chairs up all at the same time? And nobody else in the family seems concerned!)

Martha finally exploded to Jesus. "Sir, doesn't it seem unfair to you that my sister just sits here while I do all the work? Tell her to come and help me" (Luke 10:40, L.B.).

Jesus didn't rebuke Mary, but He did rebuke Martha. The Lord said to her, "Martha, dear friend, you are so upset over all these details! There is really only one thing worth being concerned about. Mary has discovered it—and I won't take it away from her!" (Luke 10:42, L.B.).

In other words, Jesus was saying, "Martha, don't fret about these things that don't really matter. There are more important things than making Me a meal. Why get so distressed about trifles? What I really came here for was to fellowship with you."

Yes, there is really only one thing worth being concerned about—our relationship to the Lord. Everything else is secondary and unworthy of our anxiety.

Is He telling us that we could live more simply, serve sliced peaches to company instead of peach pie, bread instead of hot rolls, and make time for the "one thing worth being concerned about"? Is He telling us to relax, to put first things first?

Often, in the midst of a frustration, if we asked ourselves the question: "Is this a biggie?" we would have to admit it isn't. We need to stop fussing, relax, laugh at ourselves. Praise God that the really important matters are in order.

Pericles once said in a conference, "Come, gentlemen, we sit too long on trifles." Sitting too long on trifles will not help us to *stay on top*.

Chapter 11

What Do You Expect?

"My soul, wait thou only upon God; for my expectation is from him" (Ps. 62:5).

One reason we become disappointed so often is that we expect so much from people. They don't live up to our expectations and we are crushed. This is especially true in our family life. We expect our children to be well behaved, to appreciate what we do for them. Instead, they are often naughty and ungrateful.

We expect our mates to be thoughtful, kind, considerate. A wife expects her husband to call when he can't be home on time. She expects a gift on her birthday and anniversary, to be taken out to dinner occasionally. She expects to be reassured of her husband's love by words of affection and thoughtful deeds. She expects to be appreciated.

A husband expects appreciation, too. After all, he works hard to support his family. He expects to come home to a neat house, an attractive wife, well-disciplined children, and a good dinner. He expects his wife to listen to him when he wants to talk and to leave him alone when he wants to read the paper or watch television. He expects his wife to understand his likes and dislikes, to be sensitive to his moods.

Because we are human, we fall short of these expectations. Disappointment and sometimes disillusionment result. This in turn leads to depression.

Bill Gothard urges his audiences to expect only from God, not man. If we don't anticipate attention, understanding, acts of love and appreciation from people, we will not be upset when we do not get it. On the other hand, we will be pleasantly surprised when we do.

How often when we have been disappointed by man, we are drawn closer to God. We find that only He can satisfy the deepest longings of our hearts. As the psalmist said, "My expectation is from him" (Ps. 62:5).

Sometimes even God seems to disappoint us. We pray about a problem in the home, for improvements in our health, for the salvation of loved ones. Apparently nothing happens.

A godly mother and father prayed for nearly fifty years for the conversion of one of their sons. In spite of their earnest prayers he remained indifferent to Christ and His claims. Things went from bad to worse until he became a hopeless alcoholic. His father and mother both died while he was in that state. They didn't see the answer to their prayers. Several years later, however, at the age of 53, their son was gloriously saved, delivered from alcohol, transformed into a Bible-reading, witnessing, praying, rejoicing believer! His wife, who had been in a "pit of depression" for fifteen years, was also miraculously delivered and is now bubbling over with the joy of the Lord. These parents had to wait a long time and they never saw the answer to their intercession, but their prayers were answered ultimately.

God doesn't force an entrance into anyone's life. He waits to be invited. This takes time. He is working in the life of the one for whom you are praying, bringing him to the end of himself where he will finally accept what God has to offer. But it may take many years. It may take calamities, hardships, even tragedies.

Don't be disappointed because God doesn't answer your prayers right away. Be content to wait for His time, His way. An elderly invalid woman refused to enter a nursing home even though her aging husband had great difficulty in caring for her. Nobody wanted to force her to go. The relatives prayed. Nothing changed her mind. One day the husband suffered a slight heart attack and was rushed to the hospital. The invalid woman insisted on being admitted with him. When the man was released, the doctor very naturally transferred the woman to a nursing home and surprisingly, she didn't even protest.

God has ways of working things out for us. Our part is to wait on Him, trust Him. The psalms are full of exhortations to wait on God and then expect Him to act in His way and in His time. Those who wait for Him and expect from Him are assured that they will never be disappointed or put to shame.

We must keep on expecting, then, not from man, but from God. We need to keep expecting from Him even when it seems He is doing nothing for us. Our faith will be rewarded. The answer *will come*. Our attitude of patient trust will keep us on top of our problems and difficulties.

"Mine eyes are ever toward the Lord . . . " (Ps. 25:15).

Chapter 12

Tailor-Made Just for Us

"... The Lord God had prepared ..." *(Jonah 4:6a).*

You are an important person, and so am I! Psalm 115 tells us that we "are blessed by the Lord who made heaven and earth" (vs. 15)!

Who, me? Yes, you, if you're a child of His! The psalmist says, "He will bless those who fear the Lord, both small and great" (vs. 13). I got excited when I read that the other day. We all fit into one of those categories.

In the same psalm we're told that the Almighty God, Creator of the universe, is mindful of us. When we might begin to be discouraged, think of what He has prepared for you and me: a wonderful salvation that frees us from guilt and condemnation; an eternal hope, everlasting life, and a home in heaven.

But that's not all. God not only takes care of our past and future but also our present. He even prepares the circumstances of our daily lives.

You remember the story of Christian and Hopeful in *Pilgrim's Progress*, John Bunyan's classic allegory. They were on their way to the Celestial City when they came to a stony path. They should have realized that God sometimes prepares stony paths for His children to teach them valuable lessons. They should have trusted God's love and wisdom and continued with thanksgiving and praise on the path God had prepared for them. But, like us, they forgot who had prepared the stones and began to complain.

When the pilgrims saw a smooth path running parallel to the rocky one, they decided to leave the path that led to the Celestial City and walk for a while in "By-path Meadow." The result was that they became miserably lost on the property of a horrible fiend named "Giant Despair" who locked them in a dungeon in "Doubting Castle." Only after many days of anguish and suffering did they think to pray and to praise. Then they found the Key of Promise that enabled them to escape the clutches of Giant Despair and get back on the right path again.

Disobedience always leads to despair. When we begin to stray, God prepares circumstances to bring us back to the right path again. He loves us too much to let us continue in our own way and fall into the clutches of Giant Despair.

When Jonah was running away from the Lord, God prepared a storm. "The Lord sent out a great wind into the sea, and there was a mighty tempest in the sea, so that the ship was in danger of being broken" (Jonah 1:4). Jonah was in for disaster, but without that trouble he would have been in a far worse situation—estranged from his God.

God works the same way today. When we experience a storm in our life, do we ask, "Why is God doing this to me?" Or do we ask instead, "What is God trying to tell me?" Maybe we have been walking in "By-path Meadow" and a storm is the only way in which God can bring us back to His good path. He has prepared our storms for a purpose because of His great love and concern for us. David thanked God for his afflictions because they brought him back from straying. He said it was good for him to be afflicted. He concluded, "I know, O Lord, that thy judgments are right, and that thou in faithfulness hath afflicted me" (Ps. 119:75).

God uses storms for other purposes, too. A writer on oceanography, Gordon Soule, explains how storms at sea are beneficial to sea life. Non-living matter in the sea becomes edible and nourishing when combined with air bubbles. Zoo-plankton, the tiniest of all fish, live on this food. They, in turn, become nourishment for larger fish, and so on. Eventually man benefits. And how are the air bubbles created? By storms. The violent typhoons of the Pacific and the horrible hurricanes of the Atlantic are necessary in order to create this important source of nourishment.

God prepares storms in the life of His child in order to nourish his spirit and develop his character. I recently heard the story of Freddy, a young man who had never encountered any hardships in his life. He was an oversized mama's boy. His fraternity buddies took him out to the Angeles National Forest and left him there, hoping that when he came out he would be toughened up. But Freddy never came out. A search party found his body at the bottom of the cliff. His father sadly told the authorities that Freddy was "too soft" to survive the wilderness. He said, "He never walked. We always drove him."

An old Irish blessing says, "May the wind be always at your back." That is man's way of thinking, not God's. If we never had to face a stormy wind, we would be weak and flabby like Freddy, unable to cope with the pressures of life.

We need to face the storms in God's strength. Then we can thank Him for loving us so much that He has prepared a special lesson, a blessing disguised as a storm. The prophet Nahum said, "The Lord hath his way in the whirlwind and in the storm" (Nah. 1:3).

Back to Jonah. God not only prepared a storm which resulted in Jonah's being thrown into the raging sea, He also prepared a fish to rescue the disobedient prophet. Jonah, no doubt, was not too happy with God's rescue plan, but God initiated it with the runaway's best interests in mind. Jonah needed three days in the fish's stomach to thoroughly repent from his backsliding and become willing to obey God. Oh yes, God knows what circumstances are needful for us. When the lesson has been learned, He delivers us from them. In Jonah's case, the fish got a stomachache and regurgitated him out on dry land. Immediately Jonah went to Nineveh to deliver God's message as he had been commanded.

God used Jonah to cause a whole city to repent. Because they turned to Him in genuine sorrow for their sin, God stayed His judgment. Ironically, Jonah was not pleased with this turn of events. He would have preferred to see these enemies of Israel destroyed. In anger and frustration he asked God to let him die.

Even though Jonah had obeyed God, his attitude was all wrong. He went outside the city, made a booth to sit in and sulked because things had not turned out the way he thought they should have.

God prepared a gourd to grow up over the pouting prophet to give him a shadow from the heat. Jonah appreciated this immensely. But then God prepared a worm to kill the gourd and it withered. He also prepared a vehement east wind. Now Jonah was really hot and miserable. More than ever he wished to die. But God was patiently teaching His stubborn servant. Jonah had pity on the gourd that died and on himself. What about all the people in Nineveh? Shouldn't he be concerned about them? We don't read any more about Jonah, but I hope he learned the lesson that God went to such pains to try to teach Him.

Isn't it exciting to think that the God of the universe considers you and me individually? Not only has He prepared for us salvation and a home in heaven; not only did He prepare circumstances to lead us to himself, but He prepares the events of our daily lives. He even prepares just the right home for us to be born into, the parents that are just right for us, the people that become a part of our lives.

He does this to keep us on the right path, to teach us what we need to know, to develop our Christian character, to strengthen us as Christians, to make us like himself, to accomplish His purposes through us.

Shall we not thank Him then for what He prepares for us, even if it be a stormy wind?

Chapter 13

French Toast Every Friday

"Where the Spirit of the Lord is, there is liberty"
(2 Cor. 3:17).

I didn't realize that I was set in my ways until one Friday morning when my sister, Mabel, was visiting us. "We don't need a big breakfast," she protested when I took out the eggbeater and bowl.

"Oh, but we *always* have French toast on Fridays," I answered.

I felt a bit uncomfortable as I caught a twinkle of amusement in her eye. Suddenly I felt very rigid, not only in the matter of French toast on Friday but in the other areas of my life. Already set in my ways in middle-age? What would I be like when I was old?

Right there I decided we'd have French toast on Thursdays from then on, or Tuesdays or Wednesdays. I'd have to learn to be flexible.

I realized I had also been very rigid in my work schedule. I'm one of those persons who likes to get up in the morning and get things done. I set goals for myself: This morning I'll write for three hours. Then the telephone starts ringing. Somebody drops in. My husband asks me to type a letter for him. My plans are shattered and so am I.

I'd heard of people who pray when they wake up in the morning, "Lord, I give myself to You today. Holy Spirit, guide me and use me as You want to. I'm available."

I began to pray that prayer, too, but I only half meant it. Certainly I wanted Him to use me. But would some time in the afternoon be okay? Mornings are perfect for writing and getting other things done.

With this attitude, interruptions and unexpected happenings continued to throw me. How frustrated and nervous I became. I wasn't keeping to my schedule, wasn't accomplishing my rigid goals.

Last fall at Bill Gothard's Institute of Basic Youth Conflicts we studied the subject of "rights." He posed the question, "Are you willing to give up all your rights?" He went on to ask what was that precious right we were unwilling to relinquish to the Lord.

I knew what he was talking about. Next to God and my family, the most important thing in my life was my work, my schedule, my time. God was telling me through the speaker that He wanted me to surrender this to Him. I promised Him I would. I didn't know then how soon He would test the reality of that promise.

A few days later we left Minneapolis to return home. I couldn't wait to get home and back to my schedule. I had ambitious plans to carry out, goals to accomplish. For one thing, I wanted to work on this book.

But we didn't get home. En route my husband suffered chest pains and had to be hospitalized. An arterialgram revealed three blocked arteries that needed repair. The doctor scheduled open heart surgery.

I stayed in Fargo with my husband during the

four weeks of his hospitalization. It was a far different November than I had planned. Every morning I came to the hospital and stayed until 8:30 or 9:00 in the evening.

When my husband was out of intensive care and I could sit by his bedside, I was kept busy with his needs and his visitors. I read a number of books in snatches during those four weeks and wrote many thank-you notes and letters in between my husband's naps and needs, but otherwise I didn't accomplish much according to my old standards.

One of our friends sympathized with me. "It must be hard to sit here day after day when there are so many things you'd like to be doing," he said.

To my surprise I realized it wasn't hard. God had prepared me for this enforced idleness by leading me to surrender my *time* to Him. This was how He had planned that I spend the month of November, and I was satisfied with His plan.

God taught my husband and me so many beautiful lessons through the ordeal of his surgery. One of the most precious lessons He taught me was that I could be content anywhere, doing anything, *or doing nothing.* And for an active person like me, that's really something.

I realized that even when I was sitting quietly by my husband's side, just being there, I wasn't wasting time. I was exactly where God wanted me and nothing He plans is ever wasted. I was learning precious lessons. I was fellowshiping with my Creator as well as ministering to my husband.

Psalm 91 came alive to me during those days: "He that dwelleth in the secret place of the most High shall abide under the shadow of the Almighty." I was with Him; He was with me. I didn't need to be at home bustling about accomplishing my goals. Christ was my goal.

I never dreamed that restless, workaholic me could be content in such a situation.

Now that my husband and I are back home, I'm trying to continue to practice what I learned in the hospital. I'm finding I need a lot of reviews in this lesson. Sometimes I return to my old ways and become frustrated. But when I truly relinquish my rights to myself and my time, I experience a wonderful freedom I have never known before. I know that the interruption that comes is directly or indirectly from God. In it is a lesson, perhaps, or an opportunity. It is more important than my work, my plans.

On the other hand, there are some people who have few goals in life and enjoy nothing more than just sitting around relaxing. They welcome interruptions as an escape from their work. Because they never experience the joy of accomplishment they feel useless and depressed.

The Bible does not encourage idleness. Solomon tells us to follow the example of the ambitious ant and work. He also says, "In all labor there is profit" (Prov. 14:23).

To others who tend to push too hard God says, "In returning and rest shall ye be saved; in quietness and confidence shall be your strength. . . . He that believeth shall not make haste. . . . It is vain for you to rise up early, to sit up late, to eat the bread of sorrows; for so he giveth his beloved sleep" (Isa. 30:15; 28:16, Ps. 127:2).

He says in effect, "Relax once in a while. Don't take everything so seriously. My purposes for you aren't going to be thwarted because you take an hour off for a cup of coffee and chat with a friend."

Paul said, "Where the Spirit of the Lord is, there is liberty" (2 Cor. 3:17). After many years of being a Christian I am just now experiencing that liberty that comes when we really let the Spirit of God take control.

I still have goals, but they are subservient to my own great goal—God himself and His purposes in my life.

French toast every Friday? No, not anymore. Well, maybe once in a while. I'm beginning to learn flexibility, to be free, to let God control—me, my time, everything. I still have a long way to go, but I'm on my way!

Chapter 14

Under the Circumstances

"And thou shalt be above only, and thou shalt not be beneath" (Deut. 28:13).

When someone asks you how you are, do you sometimes answer, "Oh, pretty good, under the circumstances"? The truth of the matter is that no Christian need by "under the circumstances." God intends us to be on top of them, not being ruled by them but ruling over them. He promised the Israelites through Moses that if they would obey Him they would be "above only, and not beneath."

Mrs. Charles Cowman, author of *Streams in the Desert* and other helpful books, certainly met with adverse circumstances. The illness of her husband forced them to leave their mission field in Japan. Although they attempted to aid in the work from the home base, illness soon curtailed this, too. Lettie Cowman's circumstances included sleepless nights and weary days as she cared for her invalid husband. At last Mr. Cowman died. Acute loneliness engulfed the bereaved wife. Yet she never complained about her circumstances. She refused to see anything but God's hand. She insisted that everything that came to her was part of the divine plan, God's permissive will.

Therefore, no matter how difficult, it was "just right." She maintained that she was not surrounded by circumstances but by God. *He* was her circumstance.[1]

The great Chinese Bible scholar and teacher, Watchman Nee, knew what it was to face difficult circumstances. During the years of his ministry he was often misunderstood and maligned even by Christians. When the Communists took over China and he refused to bow to their demands, he was imprisoned. During his twenty long years in a Communist prison he had this to say: "Nothing hurts as much as dissatisfaction with our circumstances."[2] He was content to suffer if that was part of God's plan for him. He maintained that nothing comes to the Christian by accident, and that nothing but good can come to those wholly dedicated to the Lord.

Twenty years in a Communist prison camp, good? Yes, if you're living "above your circumstances." Nothing can defeat a man or woman like that. God makes the "wrath of man to praise Him," turns curses into blessings.

E. Stanley Jones, eminent missionary to India, evangelist and writer, had just completed a two-month evangelistic tour of Japan when smitten by a stroke. He was 87 years old at the time. The stroke paralyzed his left side, leaving his left arm and leg useless and his sight and speech badly impaired. He could have become resentful and bitter. Hadn't he served God faithfully all his life? Why this inglorious end to his missionary career?

Instead of complaining, E. Stanley Jones recognized his adverse circumstances as an opportunity. He said with rejoicing, "God stripped me of everything to give me Everything, the last with a capital E." [3] He said to himself, "Nothing has changed; I'm the same person that I was. By prayer I am still communicating with the same Person. I belong to the same unshakable Kingdom and the same unchanging Person." [4] He could no longer preach a sermon but he could *be* one. He determined to now demonstrate what he had been preaching throughout his life. His faith was not shattered. He didn't ask, "Why, God?" He declared, "Jesus is Lord," and confidently faced the future.

It is not natural to rejoice when things go wrong, but God is calling us to *supernatural* living, lives empowered by Him to rise above the circumstances of life that bog us down in defeat.

Isn't this what Paul means when he writes of being "seated together in heavenly places in Christ Jesus"? I used to puzzle over that statement. How could I be seated up there when I was so obviously down here, quieting a crying baby, scrubbing a dirty floor, having a case of the flu?

Recently I have begun to understand the meaning of the "heavenly places" which is my position as a Christian. No, I haven't graduated from my menial tasks to a more "spiritual" occupation, but I have come to realize that my position as a Christian has nothing to do with circumstances. It is possible through Christ to live above them.

How? By accepting them as God's perfect plan for me and praising Him. Even when the washing machine breaks down. Even when the car won't start. Even when I'm swamped with too many things to do. Even when I have a headache and must entertain guests. Even when the rice burns.

Paul experienced all kinds of troubles: imprisonment, beatings, hunger, weariness, pain, disloyalty of converts. But he says while in prison, "I have learned in whatever state I am, in this to be content" (Phil. 4:11b). I'm glad that word "learn" is there. Evidently it didn't come easily, even to the Apostle Paul. But he *learned* to accept his circumstances and rejoice in the midst of them, confident that God was working out His purposes through them.

This is real freedom. This is what Paul meant in 1 Corinthians 3 when he said, "All things are yours: whether . . . the world, or life, or death, or things present, or things to come; all are yours" (vss. 21, 22). And that includes circumstances. They are ours to use, to triumph over, to be stepping stones instead of stumbling blocks.

Chapter 15

Possible Impossibility

"Count it all joy . . ." (James 1:2).

The truly amazing thing about the Christian life is that it is designed to go completely contrary to human nature. Human nature rejoices in times of prosperity and laments when adversity strikes. Nothing is more natural.

But God says that we are to value our adversities. This makes the Christian life unique and puzzling to onlookers. Paul tells us in Romans 5 that as Christians we not only glory in our hope in Christ but in our tribulations also (Rom. 5:3). Peter speaks of the trial of our faith being more precious than gold (1 Pet. 1:7). James urges us to count it all joy when we fall into various trials (James 1:2). In other words, we are not only to accept our troubles as from the hand of God, but we are also to rejoice when they come to us, recognizing them as precious gifts of God that will enrich our lives.

Ruth Hitchcock, founder of the Hebron Mission in China, learned to value the tribulations that came to her. When her mother became ill, she had to leave her work in China and take over her parents' dry-goods store which supported the work in China. As the days dragged into weeks and the weeks into years, even though she longed

to be back at her work in China, she learned to
"count it all joy." God was in control. She could
trust Him.

Finally free to return to China, she encountered the numerous disappointments and frustrations that are a part of every missionary's life, but
she had learned her lesson well. She taught the
Chinese woman who cooked for her to say in
English, "Count it all joy." With these words they
greeted one another in the morning and took their
leave of one another at night. Also, during the day
when things seemed to go wrong they repeated the
words, "Count it all joy." This attitude towards
adversity brought them triumphantly through
many a difficulty.[1]

But how can we count all joy something that is
not joyful? Maybe it's terrible! An operation, an
accident, a misunderstanding, a distress of some
kind, an annoyance, maybe even a tragedy—
count them all joy?

God's Word says, "Yes, glory in tribulations."
This sounds ridiculous until we read on and discover what trials and tribulations do for us—they
produce patience, experience, hope, endurance,
glory to God. In other words, troubles are
designed by God to develop our character and
make us the kind of people He wants us to be.

A friend of mine was concerned because she
had no troubles as many of her friends did. "I
wonder why we don't have any trials," she said.
"My husband and I are prospering financially. We
have a wonderful relationship with each other.
Our children have turned out well and have happy
homes. Everything is great." Where were the
tribulations that were designed to make them into
better Christians?

I didn't know the answer, so I just told her to

be thankful for her blessings. Later she confided to me some little annoyances in her life. Two sets of elderly parents, dear but demanding, kept her and her husband hopping. They sometimes became offended when she had time for only short visits. Often they misunderstood her and intimated she was neglecting them, even though she was doing her best to try to please them. She felt frustrated, because no matter how much she did it was never enough. Because this was such a small trial, however, compared to the traumatic experiences of some of her friends, she didn't recognize it as a tribulation in which she should glory.

It is so much easier to accept God's grace for the big trials than it is for the little ones. The Lord gave me grace recently to accept my husband's open heart surgery and even thank Him for it. But I didn't even think to ask Him for grace when we got company the other evening just as we were to sit down to supper. The guest declined the invitation to eat with us, but he lingered on while the hash got browner and browner and the hot rolls crisper and crisper. The hands of the clock kept moving and I knew we would soon be expected at church.

Not until much later did I realize that little things like dried-up hash and overdone rolls could be another way God is designing to use to teach me patience and all these other virtues He wants to work out in my life. The little irritations of each day are also tribulations in which I can glory and from which I can derive eternal benefit.

There is a sect of Buddhism that promises prosperity to its adherents. Health, financial success, happiness—all can be theirs if they faithfully follow the rules of conduct and worship.

No doubt their positive attitude brings some of these benefits to them, but, of course, eventually they are disappointed and disillusioned. In a sin-cursed world there is no way to escape from problems, troubles and suffering.

Our God doesn't promise us immunity from these things. He goes one step further and promises to *use* these very things that trouble us for our spiritual enrichment and eternal good.

How can we lose when we can actually glory in those things which are ordinarily sources of dread? What is there left to fear?

"But how can I glory in tribulation?" you ask. First, accept it as permitted by God. Believe that He has a purpose in allowing it to come to you. Thank Him for it (even if you don't feel thankful at the moment). Count it all joy! Then wait to see what God will do!

Chapter 16

Thank God You're Neurotic

"When I am weak, then am I strong"
(2 Cor. 12:10).

One of the greatest things I ever learned was to accept myself as God made me. I'm still learning it. Dr. L. E. Bisch, a psychiatrist, wrote an interesting book entitled, *Be Glad You're Neurotic.*

A neurotic, according to Webster, is a "person with a psychic or mental disorder characterized by a combination of anxieties, compulsions, obsessions and phobias without apparent organic or structural injury or change."

Dr. Bisch points out in his book that many of the "greats" of our world were neurotic. He lists as examples: Alexander the Great, Napoleon, Michelangelo, Pascal, Poe, O. Henry. He insists he is neurotic himself and delighted to be so. He states, "So famous a psychiatrist as Jung has said that all neurotics possess the elements of genius." [1]

Many of the Bible "greats" also suffered from periods of neurosis. Moses, Elijah, Jonah and Job indulged in sessions of self-pity. The disciples had their fears, Thomas his doubts. Jeremiah is called the "weeping prophet" because of his inclination toward melancholia.

Every person has his weaknesses. Even the great Apostle Paul did. But he learned to glory in his infirmities because they made him more dependent upon God and His grace.

In his excellent book, *The Spirit-Controlled Temperament,* author Tim LaHaye discusses at length the melancholic. He maintains there is a higher number of geniuses among the melancholics than any other temperament. Among these sensitive people with neurotic tendencies are musicians, poets, writers and artists. Although they have many weaknesses, as do the other temperaments, they also have their strengths. They tend to be thorough, creative, analytical, sensitive to the needs of others, self-sacrificing, conscientious and faithful.

Just as God created a variety of plants and animals to enhance our world, so He made a variety when He created people. Not only are there differences in coloring, size, appearance, and abilities among us but also in temperaments. God has permitted some of us to have neurotic tendencies as part of His plan. Not that we should give in to these tendencies, become introverted, depressed and morbid, but that we might overcome our weaknesses by His power and let Him use them to His glory.

Our weaknesses are designed to make us dependent upon Him and receive His power to live supernatural lives. Erwin W. Lutzer in his helpful book, *Failure: The Back Door to Success*, maintains that many Christians seem to be successful because they have lived apparently good lives, but are failures in God's sight. "They lived decently," he says, "but not supernaturally! They did not have the humility to see how desperately they needed God. . . . We, therefore, are pleasing to God to the extent that we apply God's grace to every experience of life." [3] Who has more opportunity to do this than someone inclined to be neurotic?

I remember times during my husband's illness when I was absolutely at the end of my own resources. I was completely cast upon God. Invariably He came across with what I needed. I realized that to learn dependency on Him was part of His plan for me. Ever since Eve took that forbidden fruit in the Garden of Eden man has been independent. We like to feel we can handle things ourselves. We don't need help from anyone.

Perhaps we can handle things quite admirably on a natural level. Many people do, non-Christians as well as Christians. They grit their teeth and take the blows of life without flinching. I saw this at the hospital when people heard of the death of their loved ones. After the initial shock often their attitude was, "I can take it. Don't feel sorry for me." Yet who knows of the turmoil on the inside that no one could see?

God has much more than a natural courage and endurance for the Christian. He gives us supernatural power. He wants to live His supernatural life through us. He wants us not only to be able to endure suffering like the non-Christians but to rejoice in it. He wants to use it as a stepping-stone to blessing and glory. He wants to display His power through us to an unbelieving world. That's why He gave us Christ to indwell us by the Holy Spirit.

Therefore, rejoice in the way God made you. If you are high strung and sensitive, thank Him for it. Thank Him for your natural weaknesses. It's part of the plan. God wants you to take by faith the power He offers to overcome your natural tendencies that are such a trial to you. As He enables you to "stay on top" people will see what He can do and believe on Him.

Chapter 17

Guilty or Not Guilty

"Christ . . . is made unto us . . . righteousness . . ."
(1 Cor. 1:30).

I was giving an object lesson at church one evening. I told the audience that I had been invited to a wedding and had nothing appropriate to wear. It wasn't the wedding of just an ordinary person, but of a King's Son. I looked at the dirty dress I was wearing. No, it would never do.

But maybe I could make a suitable dress for the wedding. I got some material together and tried my best but the result was a sorry mess—filthy rags. It didn't begin to cover me. This dirty, ragged garment would never be permitted in the King's presence.

Then I heard wonderful news. The One who had invited me to the wedding also had provided the wedding robe for me. Joyfully I put on the sparkling white robe of righteousness that He offered me. Thanks to His grace and generosity, I, though unfit in my own clothes, could now attend the wedding.

Sometimes we take that wedding garment for granted, that which cost Him His life's blood on the cross to procure for us. It is nothing less than His righteousness which He imputes unto those who will receive it. Dressed in the righteousness of the spotless Son of God, we are accepted by our holy God. It's almost too good to be true—not only to be pardoned for our past sins but to be actually clothed in His righteousness so that we can stand before the Lord blameless.

It is hard for us to grasp. We realize that although that is our position in Christ, yet in our daily lives we do sin—we fail more often than we care to admit.

A young woman married contrary to the rules of her church was excommunicated. This produced such a feeling of guilt in her that she turned away from God altogether, feeling that there was no hope for such as her. As a result she has fallen into deep depression and has had several nervous breakdowns.

A Christian psychologist and counselor told a friend of mine that he believes feelings of guilt lie at the bottom of every depression. Get rid of your guilt and you will overcome your depression, he says.

Non-Christian psychiatrists, too, are quick to attribute many emotional problems to guilt. Sometimes they try to turn their patient away from their religion altogether, maintaining that their religion has made them feel guilty and consequently they have become mentally ill.

Although unbelieving psychiatrists can often uncover the reasons for the guilt feelings of their patients, only those who believe in the blood of Jesus can prescribe an effective remedy. Thank God for Christian psychologists and psychiatrists who can point their patients to the One who can deliver them from the guilt feelings produced by sin. Jesus offers pardon and cleansing to the worst offender by virtue of His sacrifice on the cross where He paid for our sins.

In Ephesians 1:7 Paul says of Him, "In whom we have redemption through his blood, the forgiveness of sins. . . ." He has redeemed everyone. When He died on the cross, He died for all men everywhere and of all time. But everyone does not have forgiveness, because they have not availed themselves of this redemption provided for them. They choose to go on in their sins rather than to ask for forgiveness and all the blessings that come with it. They prefer to go through life and take their chances for heaven dressed in the filthy rags of their own righteousness rather than receive by faith the righteousness of Christ which alone is acceptable to a holy God.

In the film, "The Hiding Place," when Corrie ten Boom's number is called and she is about to be taken away, a fellow-prisoner to whom she has witnessed of Christ, says tearfully, "I want Him— but I don't know how." Corrie's quick reply as she leaves is, "Just ask."

It is really as simple as that. Just ask. If a person recognizes his sin and realizes his need for His forgiveness and cleansing, all he must do is ask Him. Christ will not only acquit him from his guilt but will actually impute to him His own righteousness, that "robe of righteousness" the Bible talks about.

Many times, however, after we have been forgiven our sins and have been clothed in the righteousness of Christ, we feel guilty because we sin. No one is without sin in his life. What we *do* about that sin is the important matter. 1 John 1:9 was written to Christians: "If we confess our sins, he is faithful and just to forgive us our sins, and to cleanse us from all unrighteousness."

If my child went around with a long face after I had forgiven him, I would feel sad. Doesn't he believe that I have really forgiven him? Why isn't he happy? God must feel the same way about us sometimes. Often after I ask His forgiveness for some sin I have committed, I continue to carry with me the feeling of guilt and sadness. Perhaps I subconsciously feel that if I try very hard to do something good, I will somehow atone for my wrongdoing. Meanwhile I cannot be truly free from my guilt feelings.

How such an attitude must grieve God. The Bible is full of reminders of His mercy, His forgiveness. Can't we accept it fully and freely the way it is given? If we don't, we will continue to feel guilty and consequently depressed. We can't possibly "stay on top" unless we turn our guilt feelings over to Him and believe that what we have confessed, He has forgiven.

We can't possibly "stay on top" unless we realize that we stand before God in the righteousness of Christ, and though we fail often, in Him we are blameless!

Chapter 18

Much More

"Much more, being reconciled, we shall be saved by his life" (Rom. 5:11).

My young friend had never traveled by airplane before. She decided that since the ticket cost so much, she would take a sack lunch instead of spending more money on a meal on the plane. When the stewardess passed out the dinners, my friend politely declined. Munching on her dry sandwiches she cast envious glances at her fellow passengers who were enjoying a delicious-looking hot meal. Not until later did she learn that the dinner had been all paid for when she bought her ticket. It was hers, but she didn't enjoy it, because she didn't realize it and take it.

For many years I was like that as a Christian. How I longed to be victorious and joyful as other Christians I knew. I knew there was "much more" in the Christian life than what I was experiencing, but I didn't know how I could get it. What I didn't realize was that I already had it. Rather, I already had Christ, the Source of the "much more" I longed for.

Paul talks about the "much more" in Romans 5. He tells us that Christ not only died to save us from our sins, but He lives to save us from ourselves. What He did on the cross guarantees our forgiveness. What He is, guarantees our present victory.

Ian Thomas, author of the life-changing book, *The Saving Life of Christ*, tells how he discovered this secret, "Christ in you, the hope of glory." At first he rejoiced in the fact of Christ's death for him, his salvation from hell, his hope of heaven. He zealously shared this with others seeking to win them to Christ. But all the time there was something lacking. He had not discovered the "much more."

Then, one day seven years after his conversion, Ian Thomas' life was transformed. He says of this experience, "I didn't get anything new, just discovered what I already had, Christ in all His fulness in me, 'the hope of glory.' " [1]

Christ had been in his heart since the day of his conversion, but Ian Thomas had not realized the potential of this glorious fact. Christ wanted to live His life through him. He wants to live His life through me, through you, a supernatural life in a natural world, a life that can rise above our circumstances no matter what they may be.

Watchman Nee wrote, "All the worry and fret of God's children would end if their eyes were opened to see the greatness of the treasure hid in their hearts. Do you know, there are resources enough in your own heart to meet the demand of every circumstance in which you will ever find yourself?" He goes on to say, "Why is it that some of God's children live victorious lives while others are in a state of constant defeat? The difference is not accounted for by the presence or absence of the Spirit (for He dwells in the heart of every child of God) but by this, that some recognize His indwelling and others do not." [2] Watchman Nee came to realize that his victory lay not in amassing spiritual traits such as love, but in receiving Christ in His fulness. His Christian life could be summed up after that in the word, "receive."

Madame Guyon, seventeenth-century woman of God, after much struggling, came to the conclusion that what she was seeking was within her. She prayed, "O my Lord, Thou wast in my heart, and demanded only a simple turning of my mind inward, to make me perceive Thy presence. Oh, Infinite Goodness! how was I running hither and thither to seek Thee, my life was a burden to me, although my happiness was within myself. I was poor in riches, and ready to perish with hunger, near a table plentifully spread, and a continual feast." [3]

Israel wandering in the wilderness is an illustration of many Christians. When God opened the Red Sea for Israel to pass through, the news reached the fortified city of Jericho and its people trembled. Forty long years later they were still talking about it. Rahab confessed it to the spies who came to search out Jericho. The inhabitants of the land of Canaan were no match for this powerful God, and they knew it. The trouble was that Israel didn't know it. They refused to believe in God's great power on their behalf.

Instead of entering the Promised Land flowing with milk and honey, they chose to wander in the barren wilderness for thirty-eight long years. Because of unbelief they refused to "possess their possessions."

For a long time I was like that. I accepted Christ as my Savior at the tender age of five, and in my childish way zealously served Him. During my teen years I went through a time of wandering.

I still wanted God to be there to help me in times of trouble and to take me to heaven someday, but I didn't want Him as the center of my life. *I* was the center. I was almost seventeen years old before I realized what a contradiction I was living. I saw that Christ died not only to save me from my sins but also from myself. I had no right to continue living for my own interests. I belonged to Him.

Life took on new meaning when I yielded my "self" to God. I gave Him my plans, my ambitions. I dedicated my life to Him. I told Him I'd go anywhere in the world for Him, would marry the man of His choice for me or remain single if He asked me to do that.

The Lord gave me a husband and led us both to Japan. I thought I was fully consecrated to the Lord. Hadn't I left my home, my family, my country for His sake? I didn't realize then how much more there was to surrender. I had yielded to Him in the big things, given up material possessions, home, country, personal ambitions; but I still hung on to my stubborn will when it came to my own personal life. I rebelled against submission to my husband. I chafed under disappointments. I resented interruptions in my schedule. I grumbled at my circumstances.

This was especially true when we had to send all three of our boys off to school. They came home every Saturday afternoon, but still I wept tears of self-pity on Tuesday mornings when we sent them back again.

All of these inner conflicts, these unyielded areas in my life, made me emotionally ill. I became tense, nervous, depressed. Because of this our mission board decided we should come home.

It took years of misery and a nervous breakdown before I learned that there were resources available to me that would enable me to live above my circumstances. There was "much more" than I had been appropriating. I don't mean to say I always take advantage of these resources even after I discover them (we know so much more than we put into practice). Sometimes I choose to be grumpy, dissatisfied and complaining. But I'm learning that I don't have to be. There's "much more" for me included in Christ's salvation than merely a paid ticket to heaven. There is victory over present circumstances if I am willing to accept it.

One Sunday we had overnight guests. It had been a busy day. I had planned waffles for supper. Everything was under control, going as I had planned. Then unexpected guests arrived, a family of four. Of course, I invited them for supper. But waffles for so many? With one waffle iron? Yet I had nothing else prepared.

We finally solved the problem by eating in shifts, but when I arrived at church for the evening service and hurried up to the piano to play the prelude, I was in a dither. Company was great, but company *upon* company, that was just too much. How could God expect me to take all that? I felt like having a good cry, feeling sorry for myself. I had been "put upon" and the worst part of it was that God himself had arranged it.

Then I rememberd the "much more." I remembered that Christ was living in me by the Holy Spirit. I remembered the "exceeding greatness of his power toward us who believe." The same mighty power that raised Christ from the dead dwelled in *me*. And here I was thinking I couldn't take this little extra inconvenience that *He* had planned for me.

I asked forgiveness. I relaxed. I praised God. I

didn't feel like crying anymore. I wasn't upset. I didn't have to be. I could make use of the glorious potential within me as a Christian, Christ himself in me, the hope of glory.

Ian Thomas says, "If you are born again, all you need is *what you have*, and what you have is *what* He is! He does not give you strength—He *is* your strength! He does not give you victory—He *is* your victory!" [4]

I found an article yellowed with age in a scrapbook given to me from one of my mother's elderly friends, long since in heaven. It told of a meeting in Ireland many years ago where the speaker's topic was, "For This I Have Jesus." He explained that abiding in Christ simply means that in every situation that comes to us, we can say, "For this I have Jesus," and rely on Him to see us through.

At the piano sat a young woman deeply absorbed in what the speaker was saying. Suddenly someone handed her a telegram. It was from her family telling her to come home immediately as her mother was dying. When the speaker finished his sermon and asked for testimonies, the girl stood up and told the audience about the telegram she had just received.

"My mother is dying," she said. "For this I have Jesus. I must take a midnight train and I have never traveled alone before. But for this I have Jesus."

The young woman left the meeting to take her sad journey, knowing that for this she had Jesus. Later the speaker received a letter from her. She related how she had arrived home ten minutes after her mother had died so she had no chance to speak with her. She told herself, "For this I have Jesus." The family was in chaos but for this also she had Jesus. Calmly she went about making the funeral arrangements and taking care of everything, telling herself all the while, "For this I have Jesus." She discovered that life could be an uninterrupted path of victory if in every situation she would say from her heart, "For this I have Jesus."

I read about an elderly woman who was found in her home dead from malnutrition and exposure. In her belongings neighbors discovered stacks of Social Security checks that had never been cashed.

We shake our heads when we hear such accounts, not realizing that we, too, possess unused treasures and untapped resources. We have living within us Him who is able to do "exceeding abundantly above all that we ask or think . . ." (Eph. 3:20). We have Jesus Christ in us, the hope of glory. If we will accept what He offers, we *can* stay on top!

Chapter 19

Not Everything, Something

"For who hath despised the day of small things?"
(Zech. 4:10).

I received a pathetic letter recently from a Christian woman who has suffered from depression for a number of years. Although she has spent a great deal of money on doctors and psychiatrists, nothing seems to help. She told how she could no longer do her housework or take an interest in her family because of her depression. Her children were becoming hostile, her husband threatening to leave her.

I could see it all in my mind's eye: a weepy, complaining wife and mother lying on the couch; a messy house; children having to fend for themselves; nothing appetizing prepared to eat; a disgruntled husband. No wonder they were all discouraged with the situation and looking for an escape.

Yet, having gone through depression myself, I know how debilitating it can be and how impossible everything can seem. I wrote to the woman immediately with a few homespun suggestions. First of all I told her to start thanking God for everything: her husband, children, home, spiritual blessings, and even her difficulties. Then I suggested that she start doing a little around the house every day. Obviously she couldn't muster the strength to give the house a thorough cleaning, make a delicious dinner for her family, and greet her husband at the door at 5:30 freshly bathed and beautifully coiffed. But she could do *something*. Every day she could do a little.

One day she could perhaps straighten a drawer or two. Another day she could "pick up" a messy room. Another day she would wash the kitchen floor. Perhaps one day she could manage to prepare her husband's favorite meal or surprise her children with a batch of homemade cookies.

No, she couldn't do everything, but she could do something. Even the little that she was able to do would encourage both her and her family. They would all gain hope that the situation would improve.

Sometimes our work looms before us as a formidable mountain. It helps to look at it not as a whole but in bits and pieces. One household task that has always threatened to overwhelm me is washing windows. First wash the inside, then run outside and climb the ladder to take off the combination storm window. Inside to vacuum the sill. Outside to start washing. Up and down the ladder, taking the storm windows apart, in and out, watching for streaks. And we have so many windows! Just thinking about doing them all exhausts me.

But if I decide to do only a few at a time, I don't get overwhelmed. I'll do the east side of the house this morning, another side later. It isn't nearly as hard that way. And I'm always so glad that, even if I couldn't manage them all, I did a few. Eventually I'll finish.

It's the same way with other jobs: spring cleaning, weeding the flowers, mowing the lawn, shoveling snow. If you can't face doing the whole job, do a part of it. Every small task done gives a healthy sense of accomplishment and satisfaction.

Many people become depressed because they cannot do what they used to do. This is especially true of the elderly or people who have become handicapped in one way or another.

My Aunt Tillie was always an active, busy person. She kept her home, yard and herself immaculate. She served in her church, often in a leadership role. She helped the helpless, visited the lonely, took shut-ins for rides in the country.

Now Aunt Tillis is 81 years old. She has had to move from her lovely home to a small apartment. She keeps busy caring for her seim-invalid husband. Besides that, she does little things for others as she is able. Recently she wrote, "We can't do the big things anymore, but we do *little* things." She is as cheerful and happy in her new role as she was in her former one.

Maybe we can't do big things anymore, either, but like Aunt Tillie, we can do little things. We do what we can, and we are thankful.

Maybe nervousness or some other weakness has curtailed your activities. That is not the time to give up and hibernate. That is the time to do the little things that we *can* manage. They are important, too. The Lord said through the prophet Zechariah, "Who hath despised the day of small things?" (Zech. 4:10). If God doesn't, we certainly shouldn't.

Let's get started then—in a small way at first. Maybe always in a small way. It doesn't matter how small. God will honor our efforts.

Chapter 20

Make It an Adventure

"For I know the plans I have for you, says the Lord"
(Jer. 29:11, Living Bible).

Bernice Clifton became blinded by a fall down a stairway at the height of her career as a designer decorator. At first she thought her world had come to an end until one day she heard this statement over the radio: "The worst thing that happens to you can be the best thing that happens to you—if you don't let it get the best of you." Bernice Clifton accepted the challenge of that statement. Instead of feeling sorry for herself, she got busy. At first she earned a living by baking cakes, then by typing. She learned to read Braille and obtained a seeing-eye dog. She began to lecture at clubs and churches and was soon in great demand as a speaker. Traveling widely and encouraging people from all walks of life, Bernice Clifton became fulfilled and successful. She says that her life had actually been enriched by her blindness.

Someone has put it this way: "If you get handed a lemon, make lemonade." Learn to turn your adversities into adventures!

Have you ever thought of being "broke" as an adventure? Shortly after our marriage my husband and I attended a candidate school in Chicago in preparation for future missionary work. It was a great experience, but expensive for a couple of newlyweds who didn't have much money in the first place. In a month or so my husband would continue his studies at Seattle Pacific College and we would have the G. I. Bill to live on besides part-time work. But what would we do until then?

Fortunately we had a place to live rent-free as we were "house-sitting" for relatives who went to Norway for the summer. A couple of temporary jobs helped a little. The neighbors supplied us with surplus milk they had from their cow. We also had a shelf of canned goods (with no labels), presented to my husband at a "stag shower" before our wedding. (We shook and guessed, but never knew if what we opened would be cranberries, sauerkraut or cat food!)

One day we found ourselves positively "broke." Of course we wouldn't starve; we had that milk and the enigmatic cans! We heaved a big sigh and said, "Lord, we used our money to go to that candidate school in preparation for Your work. Now what are we going to do?"

That evening when we had dinner with my husband's parents, his mother unobtrusively slipped him a five dollar bill. "Thank You, Lord!" we breathed. We were rich again. (Five dollars went further 27 years ago than they do today!)

Before we had a chance to spend it for needed groceries, however, a young couple arrived from Seattle to visit us. Good friends from Bible school, Dell had been the soloist at our wedding. We had promised to take him and his girl to Vancouver, B.C., some time (after all, he had sung for *us*).

What did Solomon say about "riches taking wings"? Yes, we could see our precious five dollar bill doing just that: gas for a 100-mile round trip, and, of course, we'd want to treat them to a meal!

There was nothing else to do, so off we went. We stopped at a fish and chips place for dinner. My piece of fish was more than I could eat, so I put a part of it in a doggy bag and brought it home with us.

Do you know what we had for dinner the next day? You guessed it: creamed fish! It tasted pretty good, too, with whatever we opened from our mysterious cans. We even had some fish left over, so I put it in the refrigerator.

Guess what we had for dinner the next day? You're right again. Creamed fish! I just added milk to stretch it a little.

Would you believe that there was still some creamed fish left over from that meal? So with a little extra milk (bless those neighbors) we had creamed fish for the third day!

I can't remember how many days we ate on that fish, but it lasted until my husband got a check and we were able to buy groceries. Remember the New Testament account of the Lord's feeding the multitude with the little boy's five loaves and two fishes? I really believe the Lord multiplied our fish, too. Our financial crisis turned out to be a glorious adventure that we wouldn't have missed for anything.

Then there was the time in one of our pastorates when our check didn't quite stretch to the end of the month. When I prepared to go buy groceries that Saturday my husband informed me there was no money. I checked the refrigerator and cupboards and told him that I could make it on five dollars this time.

"But we don't have five dollars," he announced grimly.

I gulped. We were actually "broke" and payday wasn't until next week. What would we do? We would have to depend on the Lord—like Hudson Taylor and George Muller. It was an adventure of faith. I'm not sure if I even prayed for money. I just waited to see what God would do. The afternoon mail brought a check for a story I had written (the second story I ever sold). It was for five dollars and fifty cents—five dollars for groceries and fifty cents for tithe! I *floated* to the grocery store that afternoon.

Perhaps financial difficulties are the least of our problems in these days of affluency. But we have plenty of other situations that are waiting to be turned into adventures. My nervous breakdown eight years ago certainly did. During my times in the psychiatric ward, I sometimes had a sense of this, but when depression took over, adventure was the farthest thing from my mind. This was misery and I could see nothing good in it.

Later, however, I realized what an adventure God had brought me through—a painful adventure to be sure, but one with exciting possibilities. Those miserable months of depression turned out to be the greatest learning experience of my life. I discovered God in a new way. I also discovered myself. And the adventure continues as I keep making new discoveries. I have had opportunities to share my insights with other sufferers. Learning, growing and sharing are adventures. Without problems and pain we would miss these exciting experiences with their fulfilling results.

Even my husband's heart surgery was an adventure—not a rollicking one, to be sure. But we both asked God when confronted with this serious problem, "What do You have in mind, Lord? What are You trying to teach us?" We knew

He was planning something for our good and the good of others. It became not an ordeal to be endured as much as an adventure of faith, a learning experience.

Opening my Bible and spending time with God has become an adventure. "What new truth will He show me today?" I wonder. Or what forgotten truth will He remind me of and help me put into practice?

I used to dream of exciting adventures in faraway places. Most of us don't have many of these exotic experiences. I have found, however, that for a child of God, ordinary happenings in ordinary places can become adventures if we react to what comes to us with faith and expectancy.

The little boy was selling lemonade at his box on the sidewalk, but by late afternoon the lemonade was just water—he had run out of lemons. We'll never run out of lemons, not as long as we live in this mixed-up world. What will be our attitude toward our lemons? Will we make lemonade? Will we turn our problems, our heartaches, even our failures, into spiritual adventures? We can if we will.

Chapter 21

Hope for All

"Instead of the thorn shall come up the fir tree"
(Isa. 55:13).

A young man was critically injured in a car accident. He spent months in the hospital. Finally the crisis passed. He lived, but in spite of the best efforts of the doctors, he will never be completely well again. He suffered too much irreparable damage to his body.

In the same way, some people suffer irreparable psychological damage. A young boy who has wonderful foster parents can't get over the fact that his real mother was so cruel to him she threw him down a stairway when he was an infant. Another friend of mine will no doubt always suffer from the effects of being dominated by a cruel, misguided father.

Yet, even these people can attain a certain degree of mental health. Perhaps they will be psychologically crippled until the day they die, but they need not be totally incapacitated if they are willing to change their thinking patterns and see things from God's point of view. If they are willing to accept even their tragic home situation as permitted by God for a purpose; if they are willing to accept their circumstances and disappointments as from the hand of a loving God who has only their best in mind; if they are willing to stop questioning God and believe He knows what is best for them; if they will accept the freedom from guilt He offers; if they will praise Him no matter what happens; then they, too, can enjoy a measure of psychological health they have never known before.

Even if they are not entirely well, they can accept their instability as Paul accepted his thorn—a messenger of Satan, but used of God to make Paul a humble, effective, godly person.

After the Lord had delivered me from my tunnel I was eager to talk to Norma (not her real name). She had been neurotic all her life. As she grew older she had become irrational at times and had to be hospitalized. Norma's problem was that she couldn't accept the fact that the man she loved married somebody else, and she had never found another. Her friends were all married and she was not. She felt that God had cheated her. She wondered how she could ever be satisfied and happy.

Eagerly I pointed out to Norma God's love and plan for her. He knew what He was doing in ordering her life as He had. If she would accept His will for her and start praising Him, her life could be joyous and fulfilled even if she wasn't married.

Norma, although a professing Christian, would not accept God's will for her in this matter. My advice upset her. She felt I had no sympathy or understanding of her predicament. She turned away from me. She wanted sympathy, but she didn't want help to overcome her problem. She wanted to feel sorry for herself. Although she would never say so in words, Norma is angry with

God for not giving her a husband, and she wants to stay that way.

We all know people who believed that marriage would solve all their psychological problems. It didn't. Sometimes marriage only creates a new set of frustrations. Our problems lie not in our outward circumstances, as we are prone to believe, but in ourselves. Marriage is not the answer. There are happy marriages, miserable marriages and many in between. Marriage is ordained of God, but evidently it is not His plan for everyone.

I know it isn't easy for Norma to go through life alone when she desires so much a family of her own. But is God's way perfect or not? Does He make mistakes? Does He have favorites? Does He love some of His children less than others and so deprive them of some of His blessings? We know the answers to these questions, even though we may not understand all that is involved in them.

J. B. Phillips in his book, *When God Was Man*, wrote, "A friend of mine, who is in the first rank of psychiatrists, once told me that if a patient could see and accept the love of God, his recovery would be enormously accelerated or even be instantaneous." [1]

When I complain and grumble about my lot in life, I am really saying that God doesn't love me. If He did, why would He permit my suffering? Or I am saying that He is powerless. He can't help me—that's why I'm in such a fix. To recognize at once both His love and His power—that is victory. Yes, He is powerful enough to deliver me from my suffering (Didn't He make the universe?), but He allows me to suffer for reasons I cannot always understand. He allows me to suffer, not in spite of

His love for me, but *because* of His love for me. He has a design, a plan for my life. In His great wisdom He *uses* trouble, sorrow, tragedy, evil men, and even Satan, to make my life beautiful and a glory to Him.

Should we not then praise Him for whatever He permits to come to us and for whatever He withholds? It isn't easy to do this. In fact, it is impossible when we try to do it in our own strength, but nothing is impossible with Him. He is ready to give His grace to all who will take what He offers. He is waiting to live His supernatural life through every Christian who will give Him a chance to do so. Through His power, which becomes ours through faith and praise, we will be able to overcome.

"If ye now these things, happy are ye if ye do them" (John 13:17).

Chapter 22

Don't Forget to Remember

"And thou shalt remember . . ." (Deut. 8:2).

There are three signs of old age, they say. The first one is forgetfulness. Let's see—I guess I've forgotten the other two.

Whether you're young, old or in between, you probably have been embarrassed or frustrated some time or another because of forgetfulness. You didn't remember something that was important. A minister friend of ours forgot a wedding he was to perform one Sunday afternoon. When he finally got to the church two hours late, the bride and groom had left!

The Bible is full of reminders to remember. The exiled Jews who had returned to Palestine at the command of Cyrus, King of Persia, were rebuilding the broken walls of Jerusalem under the leadership of Nehemiah. The people in the surrounding areas opposed the reconstruction of Jerusalem and tried in every way possible to stop the returned exiles. When Nehemiah learned that their enemies were planning an attack against them, he armed his builders and set them in strategic places along the unfinished wall. He said to them, "Be not afraid of them. *Remember the Lord*, who is great and awe-inspiring, and fight for

your brethren, your sons, and your daughters,
your wives, and your houses" (Neh. 4:14).

Yes, remember the Lord. Sometimes we forget
Him. No wonder we feel depressed. If we remembered Him, how great He is and that He is on our
side, it would make such a difference. Not only is
He on our side and by our side but actually living
within us by His Holy Spirit if we are true
believers. The Creator of the universe living in insignificant me! Think of it!

A man was traveling down the road, pulling in
a cart an idol that he had made. He met a Christian along the road and showed him his god.

"I made him," he said proudly.

The Christian looked at the idol, then said
thoughtfully, "I, too, have a God, but I didn't
make Him. He made *me*."

This is the God we are to remember in times of
fear and distress—the God who not only made
you and me but also everything else in the universe
and upholds it all by His great power.

He not only made us, but He *knows* us. Psalm
139 tells us how intimately He knows each one of
us. He not only knows our every action but also
our very thoughts. He knows when we are fearful,
nervous, depressed. He knows us as no one else
can, better even than we know ourselves.

The idols made by men have eyes but they see
not, ears but they hear not, mouths but they speak
not. They have hands and feet but they never move
to help anyone. In Japan, I remember seeing people bowing before their idols, clapping their
hands to gain their god's attention. We don't have
to clap our hands when we want God's ear. We
can simply call upon Him and He listens. We don't
even need to call loudly. Just a whisper, even a

silent prayer will gain His attention. Jeremiah said
in the time of his trouble, "Thou hast heard my
voice; hide not thine ear at my breathing, at my
cry" (Lam. 3:5, 6). In these days, when everyone
wants to talk and nobody wants to listen, it's good
to remember that we have a God who listens even
to our breathing when we are too distressed to
form a prayer.

Jonah remembered the Lord when he was in
the fish's stomach. Maybe we, too, remember Him
when we are in trouble more than at any other
time. Jonah said, "When my soul fainted within
me, *I remembered the Lord*" (Jonah 2:7a). When
he remembered Him, he began to pray.

One of the reasons Bible reading helps us so
much is that it causes us to remember the Lord. As
we read God's Word we are also reminded of His
mighty acts. Our faith is strengthened as we read
of His opening the Red Sea for the Israelites, of
His keeping Shadrach, Meshach and Abednego
from harm in the fiery furnace, of His protection
of Daniel in the lions' den. We see His power in
the miracles of Jesus and the apostles. We begin to
realize that such a God can solve our problems,
too, and even work miracles where they are
needed. Nothing is impossible to Him!

The psalmist Asaph was deeply depressed. He
was so troubled he could neither speak nor sleep.
He was beset by disturbing questions. Had God
forsaken him? Would he never experience His
presence and blessing again? In this unhappy state,
Asaph begins to remember. He says, "I will
remember the years of the right hand of the most
High. I will remember the works of the Lord; sure-
ly I will remember thy wonders of old" (Ps. 77:10,
11). Remembering God and what He had done in

the past brought Asaph out of his depths of depression to a place where he was able to hope again and to praise God.

The Lord wants me to remember how He has worked in my personal life in the past. Moses told the Israelites, "Thou shalt remember all the way which the Lord thy God led thee . . . " (Deut. 8:2). He went on to remind them of His amazing provisions for them as they wandered in the wilderness. He made their clothes last for forty years!

Think back on the way the Lord has led you. You can see miracles, too, can't you? The fact that He made you His child is the greatest miracle of all. Think of the little ways He has made circumstances work out for your good, how He has handled seemingly impossible situations for you, how He has taught you precious lessons through the difficulties in your life, how He has answered your prayers. Our faith is strengthened as we remember all the way the Lord has led us in the past. Will He not continue to lead us just as faithfully in the future?

I usually have my devotions in the morning before breakfast. What joy fills my heart as I "remember" the Lord and commune with Him. With Him in my thoughts I start the tasks of the day with courage and joy.

As the hours go by, however, I tend to let the cares of the day replace my thoughts of Him. "God is not in all his thoughts" was said of the ungodly in Psalm 10:4. I confess that some days God is not in my thoughts either.

Remember the parable of the sower that Jesus told? The thorns that choked the Word, making it unfruitful, were the deceitfulness of riches, the cares of this life and other things. How many times

I have permitted these thorns to choke out my concentration on Him. I start the day free and rejoicing and end it bearing a burden, because I have somehow, somewhere, let other things push God out of my thoughts. I have forgotten to remember Him. Doubts have replaced faith. Because I am not remembering Him, I am not praising, either. Perhaps I am even complaining or feeling sorry for myself.

How important it is for me to "remember the Lord" throughout the day as I work and relax, to bring every little care to Him, to praise Him no matter what happens.

In Peter's second epistle he mentions several times about putting his readers "in remembrance." In other words, he is reminding them of facts they already know, but perhaps have never put into practice.

It's easier to know something intellectually than to put it into practice in our lives. I know that God is in control, that He is leading me in every minor detail, that He is working everything out for my good. I know that if I trust Him and praise Him He will lift me above my circumstances. But sometimes the cares of life push this knowledge into the back of my mind. I find myself fretting, doubting, feeling sorry for myself. I need to be reminded again and again of the glorious truths that, if put into practice, can make me a joyous, overcoming Christian.

While I must not forget to remember, I must go a step further. I must put to *use* in my life what I remember. We all know certain truths intellectually that we have never put into practice. Have we made these principles a part of our life? David said to his son, Solomon, concerning the building of the temple to the Lord, "Be strong and do it" (1 Chron. 28:10).

He says the same to us. Don't be a murmuring, defeated, ineffective Christian any longer. You know the facts. Now then, put God's truth into practice. Do it!

I'm writing this to myself today. I have a headache this morning because I didn't sleep well last night. It's bleak and cold outside. The devil is telling me that North Dakota is unbearable in January. He is warning me that I'll have a headache all day. He predicts that cleaning the house is going to be a drag because of the way I feel. He tops it off by saying that I might as well stop writing because nobody's going to want to read this book anyway.

I can either listen to him or I can listen to God. I can push God into the back of my thoughts or I can remember who He is and what He has done in the past. I can think negative thoughts or I can dwell on His promises.

It's up to me. Not that I'm going to overcome in my own strength. I couldn't possibly. But God has already done His part. He has given me Christ in whom are all the necessary resources for victory. He is living within me by the Holy Spirit. The power is available in Him. But God won't force it upon me. I have to want it enough to reach out in faith and praise.

It works every time. I can stay on top. Yes, even when I have a headache. And so can you.

Chapter 23

Where Is Your Focus?

"Mine eyes are ever toward the Lord..." (Ps. 25:15).

Dick was so severely depressed he didn't even enjoy being with people anymore. It all started when he was in the service in Korea. Coming home hadn't alleviated his depression as he thought it would, especially when his dream of starting his own business didn't materialize. He was doing metal work for somebody else when he longed to have a shop of his own.

Dick, though not a strong Christian in those days, knew instinctively that Christ was the answer to his dilemma. One day he fashioned a crude cross out of two sticks of wood and set it in a corner of the shop behind some machinery where nobody else would notice it. When things got so tough he thought he couldn't stand them another minute, he looked at that crude cross and remembered what Jesus had done for him on Calvary. Although there was nothing magical about the wooden cross he had made, it helped him focus on Christ instead of his problems. Focusing on Christ gradually led him back to joy and peace. Today he is a rejoicing, effective Christian. (Incidentally, he now operates his own manufacturing plant.)

The reason many of us get down is that we focus on ourselves instead of on Christ. During my months of depression following my nervous collapse I regularly spent time with my Bible and in prayer as has been my habit for years. Strangely enough, I felt more depressed during these devotional times than I did at other times of the day. I couldn't understand why reading the Bible and praying depressed me. Later I understood. Even though I was spending time with the Lord I was focusing on myself instead of on Him. My devotional time had become a "self-pity party" as I told the Lord all about my troubles and my depression. He could have helped me, but I didn't give Him a chance. I wasn't even looking His way. I was completely centered on myself.

Lloyd H. Ahlem in his book, *Do I Have To Be Me?*, tells of the importance of focusing on Christ instead of self. He states: "For one seriously depressed woman I selected a series of psalms that made no reference to oneself at all. I suggested that she make no mention of herself in her prayers, simply praise God, enjoy His awe and greatness and give thanks for who He is. . . . She wasn't sure whether she was really ready to give up her own concerns and relate to God in this way. . . . Reluctantly, at first, but with increasing joy as she went along, she began to find her way out of her private emotional pit. Worship was regenerating her heart and mind." [1]

I have found this to be true in my experience also. Focusing on Christ, meditating upon who He is and His greatness does wonders for a person. Recently Psalm 115 became for me a means of focusing on Him. Reading about man-made gods of silver and gold turned my thoughts back to our years spent in Japan where we saw people all about us worshiping idols. We visited the famous *Daibutsu* in Kamakura, a Buddha as large as a building. There sits this huge work of art, a statue with eyes closed and arms folded. It could not see the people who came to worship, could not hear their prayers. Its hands never moved to help any of them.

But our God—oh, how different! He sees us in our every need; He hears our faintest cry; He moves on our behalf in answer to our prayers. "But our God is in the heavens: he hath done whatsoever he hath pleased" (Ps. 115:3). The psalmist goes on to say, "The Lord hath been mindful of us; he will bless those who fear the Lord, both small and great. . . . Ye are blessed by the Lord who made heaven and earth" (Ps. 115:12-15).

Think of it! The God who created the heavens and earth and upholds the universe is mindful of even the most insignificant of His children. When we think of who He is and then see ourselves as the recipients of His care and blessing, we can hardly stay depressed.

The writer of Hebrews says, "Consider him that endured such contradiction of sinners against himself, lest ye be wearied and faint in your minds" (12:3). In other words, focus on Him when your thinking gets confused and you start to lose your courage. Worship Him! Praise Him!

Often during my husband's stay in the hospital when I began to get discouraged, I remembered the words of David: "Mine eyes are ever toward the Lord; for he shall pluck my feet out of the net" (Ps. 25:15). As I turned my eyes on Him, I, too, escaped from the net of depression that Satan had laid for me. As I focused on Him I began to worship and praise. I was lifted out of myself and my circumstances. Joy and peace filled my heart.

If it works for me, I am confident you'll find it will work for you, too!

Chapter 24

The Destroyer

"Who redeemeth thy life from destruction" (Ps. 103:4).

A Christian psychologist who sees many disturbed people every day told me recently that he believes the problems of many of them are directly related to the oppression of Satan.

Every alert Christian agrees that we are living in the final days before the return of Christ. Satan is working overtime in a last effort to procure as many followers as possible before his opportunity is gone. We shudder at the horrors of drug abuse, accelerating crime, witchcraft and outright Satan worship.

Satan's efforts are not confined to propagating these evils, however. He is also seeking to cripple God's people and make them ineffective Christians. What better way than to tyrannize them with depression?

Sometimes depression follows or attends physical disorders. Following simple rules for health such as proper nutrition, sufficient rest and exercise could bring some out of their gloom. Others suffering from depression brought on by physical causes may need medical attention. A great many people suffer from depression, however, because of wrong thought patterns. If they could change their thinking they could get rid of their gloom.

Satan is a genius at instilling erroneous thought patterns. He started it in the Garden of Eden when he said to Eve: "Yea, hath God said, Ye shall not eat of every tree of the garden?" (Gen. 3:1). God had permitted Eve to eat of all the trees but one, yet Satan insinuated that God was withholding something good from her.

Clever enemy! He made Eve doubt God's love and wisdom. Her thinking became perverted as she listened to Satan and persuaded her husband to listen also. Man's thinking has been distorted ever since.

Why do we get nervous, worried, fearful, distressed and depressed? We can think of a dozen reasons. The children are noisy and demanding, a husband or wife is unreasonable, a friend disappoints us, teenaged sons or daughters rebel, the work piles up, the telephone rings too much, unexpected guests come, there are too many pressures, not enough money. Or, in the case of someone who lives alone, there's not enough to do, it's too quiet, the telephone seldom rings, nobody ever comes, you're forgotten, ignored, extremely lonely.

The enemy comes to us as he did to Eve and insinuates that God doesn't love us. If He did, why would He permit all these pressures to overwhelm us?

As we listen to Satan instead of to God, we become tense and nervous. We indulge in self-pity. Depression replaces our sense of well-being, sometimes to the point that we must find relief in tranquilizing drugs or hospitalization.

We need to recognize Satan for the liar that he is. Jesus called him that in John 8:44: "When he speaketh a lie, he speaketh of his own: for he is a liar, and the father of it" (KJV). If we listen to his suggestions we will be deceived. Much of the depression of my "tunnel days" resulted from listening to him and to my own changeable feelings that I unwittingly allowed him to manipulate.

Donald J. Drew suggests that instead of listening to ourselves we should *talk* to ourselves. He said in a recent address at L'Abri in Eck-en-Wiel, Netherlands: "I must really believe God and act on that belief: not listen to myself but *talk* to myself before His face and realize that what matters is *not* what I feel is true of me at any moment but what I know is true of Him at *every* moment."

Satan is not only a liar and a deceiver but also a thief. "The thief cometh not, but for to steal, and to kill, and to destroy" (John 10:10). For months I not only allowed him to deceive me but also to rob me of peace, joy, and my zest for living.

The destroyer uses various means with which to destroy his victims. Sometimes he uses the quick method of drugs, alcohol, wanton living, or the occult. He influences others to destroy themselves through wrong thinking, negativism, worry, unbelief and self-pity.

The Lord says through the prophet Hosea, "My people are destroyed for lack of knowledge" (Hos. 4:6). They had rejected God's Word, substituting for His laws their own ways and reasonings. This is what Satan wants us to do. When we listen to his lies instead of God's truth, we gradually destroy ourselves. God says, "O Israel, thou hast destroyed thyself, but in me is thine help" (Hos. 13:9). He helps us through His Word.

The psalmist says, "By the word of thy lips I have kept from the path of the destroyer" (Ps. 17:4). It is His word against Satan's; His eternal truth versus our changeable feelings.

We need not be taken in by Satan's "bag of tricks" or our own capricious emotions. We can depend on something solid and unchanging. When he comes to us with his suggestions, we can resist him with the sword of the Spirit which is the Word of God. There is no other way to stay on top.

Chapter 25

Oops!

"But as for me, my steps had almost slipped" (Ps. 73:2).

I was all ready to type this manuscript when I decided to have my husband read it and give his opinion. He deflated my ego by suggesting I needed to do more work on it.

"I've gone over it so many times," I protested. "I'm tired of it. I don't know how to change it."

"Put it away for a while," he advised. "Maybe you'll get some fresh insights."

With a reluctant sigh I gathered up my papers, stacked them in a box and put them on a shelf in the closet. Then I waited to get new insights. Instead I got the flu!

At first it wasn't too bad. I felt rather like a queen reigning from the davenport while my husband and son subsisted on peanut butter sandwiches, tomato soup and Colonel Sander's Chicken. I enjoyed catching up on my reading, just relaxing for a change, listening to records.

But after a few days I became fidgety. After reading everything in sight and answering all my letters, my eyes hurt. The house was getting dusty and nobody seemed to care. I wanted to type some articles, work on my book, clean the house, make brown bread and some good meals. But every time I got up to try these things my head started hurting again. As my fever went up my spirits went down. Back to the davenport I'd go. It became harder and harder to praise God from my horizontal position.

I had been telling others, including my convalescing husband, to give thanks for all things, even their illnesses. Eliphaz of old could have said to me as he did to Job, "But now it is come upon thee, and thou faintest, it toucheth thee and thou art troubled" (Job 4:5). Yes, it's a little different when it's *my* head that hurts and my throat that is sore.

The devil really gave me a bad time. "You've been telling others how to stay on top," he said, "and look at you. You're depressed because you've had the flu for ten days. Think of people who are ill for months or even years. You have a loving husband and son around to cheer you. Friends call and even send flowers. Think of people who are all alone in their troubles. And you're down. Shame on you! You might as well junk your book."

I did a lot of thinking. I worried, too. Maybe I didn't know what I was talking about when I insisted it was possible to overcome circumstances, to rejoice in times of suffering, to "stay on top." Maybe I was being idealistic, impractical, even unfeeling and unsympathetic.

I did a lot of soul searching. I shed some tears. I pondered the lot of people who were really suffering (not just having a prolonged case of the flu). I think now when I hear someone complain, I won't be quite so quick to judge them. I'll try to understand their struggle because I've had mine. When people who are suffering feel sorry for themselves, I'll offer them my sympathy and pray for them instead of criticizing them.

I'll pray that they will see God's loving hand in their trial, that they will realize He is working out something good for them, that they will trust and praise even if they cannot understand.

Yes, we tumble sometimes, even after we've learned how to "stay on top," but that doesn't mean we have to stay down. The prophet Micah says, "Rejoice not against me, O mine enemy; when I fall, I shall arise; when I sit in darkness, the Lord shall be a light unto me" (7:8).

God can even use my tumble to make me more dependent upon Him and to make me more sensitive to the sufferings of others.

We are perfect in Christ but imperfect in ourselves. Sometimes we will fail no matter how much "know-how" and past experience we have. God doesn't condemn us, so we need not condemn ourselves. He's there to pick us up, and give us another chance to glorify Him by our faith and praise.

Chapter 26

Happy Ever After

"The Lord shall preserve thy going out and thy coming in from this time forth, and even for evermore" (Ps. 121:8).

When I was a child I liked to read stories with happy endings. The prince married Cinderella and they lived happily ever after.

Our story isn't finished yet. My husband is making a good recovery from his heart surgery and is back at his preaching and other work. He is playing golf again and engaging in other exercise as others are doing who have had the same surgery. So things are looking brighter. Our story, so far, has a happy ending. But will it stay that way?

I'm sure we can expect more troubles, possibly more surgery, maybe illnesses of various kinds as we grow older, and perhaps other difficulties in the future. We will, no doubt, experience our share of disappointments, failures, hardships, loneliness and pain, which is a part of life on this earth. We may even have to face acute suffering such as others in our world are experiencing: famine, privation, prison, torture, death.

Of course we shrink from the thought of such things, but God has promised the grace to overcome if that time should ever come. Meanwhile He

126

wants us to trust Him in the lesser difficulties and
trials that He permits, to see His love in everything
that comes to us, to praise Him even when things
look dark, to rejoice and be happy in Him. When
we think of what He has done for us in the past,
what He is doing for us now if we are permitting
Him, and what He has in store for us in the future,
should it be so hard to rejoice?

Can we stay on top? Is it possible? Why not?
God is willing to make it happen if you and I are!
Not in our own strength, but in His!

"Now thanks be to God, who giveth us the victory through our Lord Jesus Christ" (1 Cor.
15:57). And that's not only for now but for eternity!

Notes

Chapter 1, In and Out of the Tunnel
1. Hannah Whitall Smith, *The Christian's Secret of a Happy Life*, Fleming H. Revell, p. 143.

Chapter 2, Greet the Dawn with Song
1. B. H. Pearson, *The Vision Lives*, Christian Literature Crusade, p. 61.
2. Source unknown.
3. F. J. Roberts, *Come Away My Beloved*, King's Press, p. 3

Chapter 4, The "If Only" Game
1. This article was printed in *Evangel*, Light and Life Press. Used by permission.

Chapter 5, God Did It
1. Madame Guyon, *Madame Guyon*, Moody Press, p. 114.
2. Ibid., p. 367.
3. Ibid., p. 381.
4. S. I McMillen, *None of These Diseases*, Fleming H. Revell Co., pp. 69-72.

Chapter 6, God's Point of View
1. B. H. Pearson, *The Vision Lives*, Christian Literature Crusade, pp. 72, 81, 134.
2. Elisabeth Elliot, *These Strange Ashes*, Harper and Row, p. 129.
3. Howard and Phyllis Rutledge, *In the Presence of Mine Enemies*, Fleming H. Revell.

Chapter 8, Thought Control
1. John Barbour, "Mind Control," Minneapolis Tribune, Nov. 1966.

Chapter 9, Questions, Questions
1. Flannery O'Conner, *Mystery and Manners*, Farrar, Strauss Giroux, p. 227.
2. Elisabeth Elliot, *These Strange Ashes*, Harper and Row, pp. 110, 111.
3. Angus Kinnear, *Against the Tide*, Christian Literature Crusade, p. 92.

Chapter 14, Under the Circumstances
1. B. H. Pearson, *The Vision Lives*, Christian Literature Crusade, pp. 81, 134, 165.
2. Angus Kinnear, *Against the Tide*, Christian Literature Crusade, p. 174.
3. E. Stanley Jones, *The Divine Yes*, Abingdon Press, p. 25.
4. Ibid., p. 31.

Chapter 15, Possible Impossibility
1. Ruth Hitchcock, *The Good Hand of Our God*, David C. Cook Co.

Chapter 16, Thank God You're Neurotic

1. Louis E. Bisch, M.D., *Be Glad You're Neurotic*, McGraw Hill, p. 4.

2. Tim LaHaye, *The Spirit-Controlled Temperament*, Tyndale House.

3. Erwin W. Lutzer, *Failure, the Back Door to Success*, Moody Press, p. 47.

Chapter 18, Much More

1. Ian Thomas, *The Saving Life of Christ*, Zondervan, p. 122.

2. Watchman Nee, *The Normal Christian Life*, International Students Press, pp. 99-101.

3. Madame Guyon, *Madame Guyon*, Moody Press, p. 72.

4. Ian Thomas, *The Saving Life of Christ*, Zondervan, p. 70.

Chapter 20, Make It an Adventure

1. Bernice Clifton, *None So Blind*, Rand McNally.

Chapter 21, Hope for All

1. J. B. Phillips, *When God Was Man*, Abingdon Press, p. 19.

Chapter 23, Where Is Your Focus?

1. Lloyd H. Ahlem, *Do I Have To Be Me?* Gospel Light Publications, p. 200.